THE WISDOM OF THE BENEDICTINE ELDERS

THE WISDOM OF THE BENEDICTINE ELDERS

Thirty of America's Oldest Monks and Nuns
Share Their Lives' Greatest Lessons

MARK W. McGINNIS

Cover design by Cynthia Dunne
Text design by ediType

Please note: Some Benedictine communities spell out the word "Saint" that they carry in their name, while others use the abbreviation "St."; for reasons of consistency, the abbreviated version "St." is used throughout this book.

Library of Congress Cataloging-in-Publication Data

The wisdom of the Benedictine elders : thirty of America's oldest monks and nuns share their lives' greatest lessons / [edited by] Mark W. McGinnis.

p. cm.

ISBN 0-9742405-3-2

1. Benedictines – United States. 2. Monastic and religious life – United States. I. McGinnis, Mark W., 1950- II. Title.

BX3003.W57 2005
271'.102273 – dc22

2005002349

Published by

BlueBridge

An imprint of United Tribes Media Inc.
240 West 35th Street, Suite 500
New York, NY 10001

www.bluebridgebooks.com

Printed in the United States of America

10 9 8 7 6 5 4 3 2

Dedicated to the thirty wonderful individuals whose thoughts, lives, and faces fill the following pages

CONTENTS

FOREWORD

In the opening stanza of his "Choruses from 'The Rock,' " T. S. Eliot laments the great loss of meaning in our modern times. What we perceive as vast knowledge is in fact mere data, unawareness, and, ultimately, destruction. "Where is the wisdom we have lost in knowledge," he wails, and the sound of this haunting question echoes through time. In our era, in fact, that question may have now become more important than ever.

We are immersed in the greatest information explosion since the beginning of time. We communicate around the globe in seconds, we research the ages at the click of a computer mouse, we scan and file the history of generations on handheld devices and play them back on CD-ROMs. No doubt about it, we have information aplenty. We know about atoms and quarks, about lasers and computers, about both the moon and Mars, about nuclear fusion and nuclear fission, about holographs and MRIs, about genes and DNA. We can compute and measure and explore and decode and destroy at the touch of a button. We are the information giants of human history. What we do not know, far too often unfortunately, is what to do with all these facts and things — and why.

Where, indeed, is the wisdom we have lost in knowledge?

Knowledge gives us information. Wisdom gives us light on the way. Knowledge is a skill. Wisdom is a quality. Knowledge can be learned. Wisdom can only be distilled from those places in life where knowledge was not enough to really explain what was happening to us, or information failed to resolve what was happening to the other.

The problem is, if truth were known, that knowledge is not ever enough to really answer the questions under the questions, and wisdom is demeaned for answering them without fact. "You don't know anything about that," we are fond of saying in this generation. "You are out of touch," we remind those who do not own a computer, who have no cell phone, who have no desire to surf or search or blog. Such people are "past their prime," have "missed the moment," are "over the hill," this culture insists. They "live on a different planet," one long past, one long gone.

Over half the population of the world, excluding the populations of North America and Europe, is under the age of fifteen. The West itself, thanks to the new global consumerism and its discovery of the youth market, is increasingly child-oriented. Age, once touted by the Greeks as the ultimate acme of knowledge, is now an anachronism. It wearies us.

Western society, in fact, has made age the blight of the time, ageism a sign of progress, not intentionally, perhaps, but certainly effectively. In a culture that defines people by what they do — the first question asked of a person in the United States after their name — people who used to work as managers or skilled employees into their seventies are now encouraged to retire as young as fifty-five. But "retirement" in a production-oriented society is the kiss of death that marks a person in such a society unimportant, doddering, useless.

No wonder that in the West both men and women spend a great deal of money and time to look younger than they are, act younger than they are, become younger than they are. Exercise trainers, hair implant specialists, fad diets, plastic surgery, and body-building have become the science of youth while around the globe people die from the violence of poverty and the ruthless use of power because the world lacks the wisdom to deal with the knowledge it has spawned.

Our knowledge has run away with us while our wisdom has been sacrificed to age discrimination and the cult of youth.

And where shall we go to find another way? In fact, is there such a way, and, if so, where is it?

The truth is that the West itself gave birth to another tradition, still alive, still dynamic, that reverences age and seeks wisdom more than knowledge. The fruits of this tradition are what *The Wisdom of the Benedictine Elders* explores.

The Rule of Benedict, an ancient spiritual document from the sixth century CE, embodies both the antidote to ageism and a model of wisdom-seeking to which Confucius referred five hundred years before Jesus when he said, "By three methods we may learn wisdom: First, by reflection, which is noblest; second, by imitation, which is the easiest; and third, by experience, which is the bitterest." The process of reflection, imitation, and experience is built into Benedictine life.

The monastic spends hours every day immersed in the Scriptures, listening to the Word, learning from her mentors, and exposed to the demands of life. What's more, in Benedictine life, no one ever "retires." I remember, as a young sister, reading two passages of the Rule that gave me pause. The first excerpt required that the prioress or abbot take advice from everyone in the monastery, from youngest to oldest, "whenever weighty matters are to be decided," as the Rule put it. *But how would the old sisters know what to do, I thought, when they hadn't been in any kind of professional position for years?*

The second passage was even more difficult for me to understand. "Even the ill and the elderly are to be given a task," the Rule required. I was astounded by the harshness of the precept. *Why would you expect people to go on working in the monastery,* I wondered, *when they were either ill or old?*

It took me years to get the message: In a Benedictine monastery, no one is ever useless. No one is ever out of the center of things. No one is ever discounted. Wisdom is the essential quality of life to be cultivated here, not simply skills or devotions or degrees. The Rule of Benedict itself is a piece of wisdom literature. It concentrates on the major questions of life, not on the mechanics of life.

This book sets out to tap the roots of that wisdom.

When I was prioress of a community in transition from a stable form of institutional ministry — teaching — to a more extended form of individual ministries, I worried that young people who would no longer likely be living and interacting daily with our older members would never truly get to know them. So I instructed our formation team to see that one of the community works that fell to each new member would be to clean an older sister's infirmary room. It wasn't that we didn't have a good infirmary staff to do such things. It was simply that cleaning was really not the goal of the exercise. And sure enough, on Saturday mornings as I walked the halls, I passed room after room where a young woman sat on the floor cleaning out drawers while the older sister whose room it was regaled her with stories about the past, about life, about spirituality, about human growth, about the ways of God with the world — about the wisdom these elders had culled from years of reflection on the Scriptures, learned from the sisters around them, struggled through in their own lives. It was all about a wisdom quest.

Now, thanks to *The Wisdom of the Benedictine Elders,* voices like these will live on for all of us to hear. Their messages are clear: they speak of faith in God, of service to many, of happiness in the community, and of openness to life. They expose the cancer of ageism, they bring new attention to the insights of life, they warn us of putting too much stock in the accoutrements of life. They bring us their physical frailties clothed in the strength of the spirit.

The book itself is a wise one. May it engender in all of us the wisdom to ask what we are missing by failing to recognize what the Greeks took for granted, the wisdom of age. Or as the book of Proverbs put it long before T. S. Eliot:

> Happy is the one who finds wisdom,
> and the one who gets understanding,
> for the gain from it is better than gain from silver
> and its profit better than gold.
> She is more precious than jewels,
> and nothing you desire can compare with her.
> Long life is in her right hand;
> in her left hand are riches and honor.
> Her ways are ways of pleasantness,
> and all her paths are peace.
> She is a tree of life to those who lay hold of her;
> those who hold her fast are called happy.

Joan Chittister

INTRODUCTION

This book began as a labor of inquiry and ended as a labor of love.

As an artist, I frequently approach a subject matter in the form of a series of paintings. Examples of this approach are my two series, *Lakota and Dakota Animal Wisdom Stories* (1992) and *Buddhist Animal Wisdom Stories* (2002). More recently I created a project of 103 small paintings based on Rabindranath Tagore's 1913 collection of poetry, *Gitanjali.*

Back in 1995, I produced the project *Elders of the Faiths,* in which I met, and then painted, fifteen elders of various religious backgrounds who live in my home region. One of the elders in this 1995 project was Sister Marie Kranz of Sacred Heart Monastery in Yankton, South Dakota. I was very moved by her deep wisdom and knowledge. Over the years I have also met other sisters of Sacred Heart Monastery (through my work with the South Dakota Peace and Justice Center) and have consistently been touched by their dedication to helping others.

Also in the mid-1990s, I began to go on personal retreats to Blue Cloud Abbey in northeast South Dakota. These retreats deepened my interest in the Benedictine way of life. Among the monks I found a tremendous diversity of personalities and attitudes bound together by a true sense of devotion. My connection with the monastery became so meaningful that in the late 1990s I applied and was accepted as an oblate, a lay member of the community. As an oblate, I attempt to use the

Rule of St. Benedict as one of the guiding lights of my life, and several times a year I retreat to Blue Cloud to rest, meditate, sketch, and join in the rhythm of the monastery.

All of these encounters made me want to know more about the Benedictines in America today, fifteen hundred years after Benedict of Nursia first wrote his famous Rule. I wanted to learn about the everyday rhythm and ritual of prayer and work, about the solitude and community, sanctity and humor in monastic life; and because so often it requires personal experience to gain deeper understanding, I decided to undertake an art project and to create a book that would enable me to meet thirty elders of the Benedictine order, nuns and monks who were born between 1901 and 1925 and who are at home in monasteries and convents across America.

I began to contact Benedictine communities wherever my travels would take me, and I also made two month-long sweeps of the country specifically to meet the elders. The abbots and prioresses of all these communities were kind enough to welcome me and my wife, Sammy, who often accompanied me, as their guests. In most cases they, or the monastery's or convent's council of elders, selected the representative of the community with whom I would meet for my project. I spent many hours in conversation with each elder, recorded our conversations, and also took pictures of her or him and the monastic setting as visual aids for my portraits. Back in my studio I would then create both the painted and the written portraits.

My conversations with the elders focused on the moral, spiritual, and everyday aspects of their long lives. They shared with me when and why they decided to enter the cloistered world; how the Benedictine Rule and tradition serve as foundations for their spiritual and physical lives; their celebration of the spirituality of everyday objects and chores; their moments of greatest joy and deepest sorrow; if they ever had, or still have, any regrets about the path they chose; and their hopes for the future.

After I transcribed our recorded conversations and my handwritten notes into manuscript form, I sent a copy of each text portrait to the elder for her or his review.

The paintings are not an attempt to give a photographic likeness of the elders. They are an interpretation of my experiences with each elder and his or her monastic community through my painting style. Many people today are conditioned by studio photography portraiture that often presents a rather sanitized image of the sitter. My approach to portraiture is based much more in naturalism and an attempt to show key aspects of the character of each individual as I experienced her or him. My portraits of the elders attempt to express the diversity of qualities I found in each of these remarkable individuals: kindness, seriousness, intensity, gentleness, intelligence, and sincerity are all qualities I much hope are reflected in the faces I have painted. Each portrait is also filtered through my painting style of heightened textural and color qualities, which creates a personalized representation.

I began this project in the hopes of finding a better understanding of the Benedictines, and I think I have succeeded on a beginning level. At the same time, I have learned so much more. I became deeply impressed with the attitude of sisters and brothers toward their fellow Benedictines and toward outsiders. It made me think much more deeply about the way I treat others — my students, my family, my friends, even strangers. There is so much in Benedictine life that is a marvelous model for the lay world: hospitality and charity without question, devotion to ideals, deep listening, humility, valuing silence, moderation in food and drink, reading for growth, open-mindedness, an unquenchable desire to learn, and an elevation of the spirit. These are just a few of the outstanding Benedictine qualities I encountered again and again, and they are qualities I would very much like to develop more fully in my own life.

The Benedictines have taught me a new dimension to my understanding of love — an unconditional love that does not discriminate about who you are, what faith you have, or even why you have come to them. It took me a while to understand that this is simply the love of God in practice. This love was so apparent in the elders I met, and in an exemplary way in the late Father Frederic Schindler of Mount Michael Abbey in Elkhorn, Nebraska. I was not able to put into words my experience with Father Frederic until I met Abbot James Jones of Conception Abbey in Conception, Missouri, some days later. When I mentioned to him that I had recently spent time with Father Frederic, Abbot James simply said, "Yes, Father Frederic . . . he is a transparently good man." It was the perfect description.

This transparent goodness was a quality I found again and again in the wonderful women and men I was fortunate enough to meet and spend time with (some of whom, sadly, have since passed away). It is my great hope and wish that through this book their lives, and their wisdom, will be shared with others.

Mark W. McGinnis

Father

STANISLAUS MAUDLIN

Born 1916

Father Stanislaus is a member of the Benedictine community at Blue Cloud Abbey in Marvin, South Dakota.

❂

Blue Cloud Abbey is where I begin my visits for this book. Naturally so, since I have been coming to this monastery for some years for personal retreats — escaping my beloved but at times too-persistent students, the university administrators, the ever-encroaching bureaucracy, and even my studio, where I tend to become somewhat obsessed. The abbey, perched high over the pastoral farmland of the Whetstone Valley, gives one a feeling of clearer perspective and calm. My growing fascination with the lifestyle of the monks and the remarkable diversity of individuals I have found at Blue Cloud has been a major inspiration to create this book. Father Stanislaus ("Stan") is the perfect representative of the community; he is one of the founding monks who helped build the monastery in 1950, the year of my birth. Blue Cloud was founded by St. Meinrad Archabbey (in southern Indiana) to serve the American Indian people of North and South Dakota.

I have an unusual experience creating Father Stan's portrait. When I am done, I set the painting on my easel for contemplation — and in a flash I realize that I am looking at the face of my late father. I have never noticed the startling resemblance before, neither in all of my encounters with Father Stan, nor in the long process of painting the portrait. Is this yet another reason I am so drawn to the abbey?

Today, after more than a decade of frequent visits to the Blue Cloud community, and after I joined them as an oblate, I have developed a deep affection for the place and its people. It has become a very important part of my life that I am most thankful for.

Father Stanislaus

My father was a generous man and a dreamer; he had many ideas of doing great things for the family and for others. He worked as a clerk in a clothing store in Indiana at the time of my birth. In 1927, he followed through on a dream to start his own clothing store in the same small town. By the fall of 1928, he was forced to close the store and go into bankruptcy. Going bankrupt in those days meant losing everything. We were allowed to stay in our home a few weeks, but then we were asked to leave and were homeless. My Aunt Gail, who had helped take care of much of her family all her life, had recently decided she would become a nun. When Aunt Gail heard that we were in need, she put aside her own wishes, insisting that we come and live with her. We started out on our trip to Aunt Gail's house about thirty miles away. On the trip, we were going down a long hill and at the bottom my father had to stop the car as he was crying too hard to drive. I had never seen my dad cry before; he was always smiling and joking. But he cried and sobbed that he had let his family down. Mother was sitting beside him and shifted the newest baby to her right arm and slid over and comforted him. After a time, Dad wiped his eyes and we went on. If I could find that Indiana road today, I would be able to show you the exact spot where it happened. This was the low point in our family's fortunes; we began a slow rise after that. Aunt Gail took us in and planted a bigger garden, and we ate what vegetables she could grow. She ended up caring for a group of my cousins as well. Dad worked odd jobs but could find no regular employment. My mother's poor health was also a burden.

I was in the seventh grade in the Catholic school. Our pastor annually had a week of special sermons for the parish. In 1929, we had a Franciscan priest. Our teacher, Sister Corona, took our grade over to the church in the afternoon to listen to him. I thought he was boring. The only thing that interested me were the cold red toes poking out of his sandals. He furiously exercised them, trying to keep them warm in the chilly church. But then he said something that made sense. While waving his arms he said, "Boys and girls, I want to guarantee you two things, if you do one." I liked the word "guarantee," and I liked the small number, "one." He pointed to a large stained-glass window in front of us. In the center of the window was a triangle that even then I understood as a symbol for God. He said, "This is all I ask you boys and girls to do. When you come to church you look up to God and say, 'Here I am, God. I am strong, healthy, brave, and ready. Any time you are in trouble and need something done, let me know and I will do it.' " The priest looked at us and said, "If you do this one thing, I guarantee that you will always have a job and love every minute of it." I thought I could do that, and resolved to do it every Sunday. But at that age I was also forgetful, and maybe only once did I actually come into church and look up at that symbol and say, "Here I am, God. I'm strong, healthy, brave, and ready. Any time you need something done, I'll do it." I just forgot.

I was a healthy seventh-grade boy with a girlfriend. I also had a best friend who had just decided to go to the seminary at St. Meinrad, Indiana, to study to be a priest. I didn't want to lose such a good friend, so I decided to go with him, study, and leave when I felt like it. I told my mom, and she was delighted and wanted me to tell our priest immediately, but I was afraid to. Finally I did tell him. He was pleased and offered to let me skip the eighth grade and he would tutor me so I could start at St. Meinrad in the fall. Now it was just a month and a half earlier that the Franciscan priest had said, "Say yes to God and you will always have a job and love every minute of it," and events had already begun to spin, and the spinning continues to this day. Well, my best friend's parents forbade him to go to St. Meinrad, making him finish the eighth grade. I went to St. Meinrad with a suitcase of new clothes provided by a local Jewish businessman from the goodness of his heart. The rules at the seminary were very strict, and all rules were followed to the letter or you were dismissed with no questions asked. The bishop and my local priest were paying my tuition. I was so poor I could not even go on field trips, as I couldn't afford the extra fees. I grew very attached to the monastery but continued to plan on becoming a priest and being assigned a parish and not becoming a member of a monastic order. (One of the teachers once casually mentioned that I should join the monastery and stay.)

In the middle of my education it was announced that the bishop was bankrupt and any of us who were supported by him should take all our belongings home at Christmas, as we would not be coming back. I was lying in bed the night before going home for the holidays when I was summoned to see the rector. He said that he had heard I wanted to join the monastery. It was news to me, as I had never even thought of it. He told me that I could come back after Christmas, as the monastery would pay my tuition. This is how the spin happened: once I had said yes to God, everything followed course. In 1934, I had my head shaved, clothes changed, diet rearranged, and I entered as a novice at St. Meinrad Abbey.

One day in 1937 after dinner, I was instructed to walk with the abbot. He said that the seminary needed more teachers.

He said they were sending me to Rome to get two degrees. In those days the superior was not expected to say, "Do your best, try hard, we hope you make it." He gave a simple command: "You will get two degrees, a doctorate in theology and a minor degree in scripture." He said, "Tell your folks you will be gone for seven years, at least." Before I went to the train station to leave for Rome, my father called me aside and gave me a blessing. It was the only blessing I ever received from him, and I'm still walking in the power of that blessing nearly seventy years later.

I loved every minute of Rome, but being young and foolish I worked obsessively at my studies, not eating well, and not taking the exercise I should have. I became ill, and then in 1939 all Americans were ordered out of Italy due to the war. I arrived back in Indiana in March of 1939. They took one look at me and told me I was no good to them around there. They sent me off to the Dakotas, and I have been here since. I have told this story to others and it has been said to me that I never really had a vocation, I simply fell into it. And it's true, I have simply said yes to what needed to be done and did it. In my work at Turtle Mountain Reservation in North Dakota, if we needed a basketball coach, I became it; if we needed a scoutmaster, I was it. It didn't matter that I knew nothing about it. I got books and started reading.

I was later appointed superior at St. Michael Mission in North Dakota. I was a total failure. I am a person who is meant to be with people and not behind desks writing letters and managing. After seven years and many requests from me, I was transferred to take care of three churches in central South Dakota. They were about seventy miles apart, and each needed attendance every Sunday. I eventually received some help and spent ten wonderful years living near the dump in Pierre, South Dakota, where the poor people lived. I never locked my door in ten years. Since then I have had numerous jobs, including starting the American Indian Culture Research Center here at Blue Cloud. All the things I have done relate back to just saying yes to God for what he needs. I have been told that people take advantage of me. My response is that I hope they will. I hope I can give advantage to people. That's not out of the ordinary for any Christian. Jesus calls us to spend ourselves, not conserve ourselves. Remember that the Creator asks only one thing of us, that all creatures say yes. After that the future is planned by the Creator. It's like the joining of the egg and the sperm. In an instant, it is all in the genes. As the cells multiply, the imprinted information naturally develops.

My primary duties in the order have been twofold, and they are very important to me: work and prayer. Work to me means service to others. It is not primarily mental work, choosing a course of study. Work for me means saying yes to immediate needs of people. My work inspires my prayer; my prayer energizes my work. These two are like the two feet under a human being, first one step, then the other, and so on. When one pays attention to both work and prayer, one can stay in very good balance. The Creator gave us one imperative in early Genesis. He said "work." Make this a better world, try to restore it to its pristine beauty, make this a creation of balance among all of God's creatures. Most of my work has been carried out by being partners with American Indian people. I have been given an Indian name five times by different groups I have worked with, as a way of being baptized into their circle. Some of the names have been a bit lighthearted, such as one community that had one of their first encounters with me as I made a spectacular fall, slipping on the ice. The name they bequeathed to me translated to "Graceful Walker." Other names were more serious, such as the name given me at Turtle Mountain that translated to "The Eagle That Blesses."

A hazard in being a servant is that onlookers feel free to criticize the servant. Accepting criticism is part of being a servant. Criticism comes most directly when one is seen as a servant to minority groups. Majority people criticize you firstly because you are serving "those" people, and secondly because you're not serving them by trying to make them white. If you are a servant, you put up with criticism and don't let it derail you. In my work I have tried to help non-Indian people to understand the philosophy, spirituality, and worldview of Indian people, and with this understanding gain respect for Indians. It's a goal that may never be reached, but it's like the North Star; it's there to guide you.

I have had many joys in my Benedictine missionary life. My time in Rome was a high point, and my years at Turtle Mountain were very meaningful. I feel a great affinity to the Turtle Mountain people. My time in Pierre, and my nearly thirty years now at the American Indian Culture Research Center here at Blue Cloud, have had many periods of joy. I think it's better to have a life that is measured rather than a life that has many highs and therefore also many lows. But overall the greatest joy in my life has been my identification and oneness with Indian people. And my greatest sorrow was when it became evident that I could not return to Turtle Mountain, to finish out my life there. When it was decided that the Benedictines should leave Turtle Mountain it was a deep sorrow to me. My every thought is still with the people there, and I continue to pray that I might go back and retire there as an elder in the community. But as I reflect, I begin to feel that part of the problem is that for the first time in my life I asked for something on my own; I tried to plan. Planning has never been the way my life has taken its course. I have said yes to whatever event offered itself to me. Planning has not been a part of it.

I feel that Benedictine men and women of today have not yet fully and deeply claimed the wisdom of Benedict. In spite of themselves they are the products of this competitive consumer society. Even in their spiritual lives they talk of gaining merit, they talk of gaining heaven, they speak of earning rewards, and they talk of planning the future, of knowing what "they" want. This is a result that must be guarded against in communities. Community can settle at the lowest common denominator. Benedict warned against it. Nearly every page of the Rule of St. Benedict is some kind of psychological insight on the dealings of human beings. I truly believe that there has been no wiser person writing a Rule. Benedict's Rule is not just a manual; it is a statement of living. My direction in the tradition has been one of service, of saying yes. It is a tradition of mutual help. The Creator made men and women so that when they serve each other, they create new life. When two people have a covenant with each other, the result of that covenant is always a new creation.

One aspect of the Rule is stability; that means perseverance, or even stubbornness. Once you've started a job, do it. Don't let your energy be deflected by other conflicting interests. An important part of the tradition is contained in the first word of the Rule: "Listen!" Listen to the sounds of creation: the wind, the trees, the animals, the people. Another concept that is important to me in the Rule is humility, humble, human, humus, the earth. Be like the earth absorbing everything, and having absorbed everything send up new flowers, new creation, new fruit, new beings. I like to take things in their simplest form. Benedict by his few words makes things very simple for me. I wish I could make things simple for people as well. We live in such an artificial and complicated society. When I give retreats, I try to help people relax and recognize the simplicity of life and the simplicity of our commitment to the plan of the Creator.

I had a wonderful beginning with my parents. I think the monastic life has simply reinforced what my dad and mom started: respect for others, politeness, helpfulness, attentiveness, obedience, and prayerfulness. I now feel that it is also important to try to get people to listen to nature, to the Creator. It's sad, I think, how people study so frantically the wisdom of humans but are not able to pay attention to the wisdom of creation. Simplicity and listening are a large part of that wisdom, being close to the Creator through the things that he has made. Listen to the sky, sun, sleet, wind, rain, and animals. At last, some people in science are beginning to see that everything is fundamentally spiritual. At one time scientists thought the atom was the smallest component of matter, then the quark. Now they know there is something even smaller. Someday they will have to see that it is all spiritual. The Indian people see this clearly and could teach it to us all, if we would listen. Most people are too divorced from the earth to see the presence of the spirit in all that is around us: the spirit in the rock, the fire, animals, the water, the spirit in all creation.

My hopes for the future are that, having said yes and continuing to say yes, the future will be as it must be in the hands of the Creator.

Sister

VICTORINE FENTON

Born 1920

Sister Victorine is a member of the Benedictine community at Mount St. Benedict Monastery in Crookston, Minnesota.

An outstanding feature of Mount St. Benedict Monastery, at least among the monasteries I have visited, is its vegetable garden. Whenever I would compliment a monastery on its fine garden, the members there would say, with typical Benedictine humility, "This is nothing, you should see the garden at Crookston." And it is a sight to see, with plot after plot of well-tended vegetables bordered by fruit trees. The varied greens of the different vegetables create patterns and rhythms in their well-tended rows. The pumpkins and squash bulge out from the canopy of vines and leaves. The limbs of the apple trees are burdened with the weight of the apples ready to be transformed into sauce, jelly, and pie. There is a wonderful feeling of bounty to the garden, a bounty the monastery generously shares with those in need in the town. Like all the sisters her age, Sister Victorine spent her fair amount of time tending the garden in her younger years. She is a wonderful example of the flexibility displayed by so many Benedictines, always ready to use her talents and to expand her talents for the good of the community. From her early days teaching, to her ten years as prioress in the turbulent days of Vatican II reforms, to receiving her doctorate at the age of sixty-five, her learning and growing for the benefit of others are simply a way of life.

Sister Victorine

MY FATHER HAD attended school at St. John's Abbey in Collegeville, Minnesota, and I think he was really a monastic at heart. He was a baker and also an artist at his craft. He did wonderful things in his baking and decorating. We moved around a great deal in my childhood, but in the eighth grade I began going to a school that was staffed by sisters from here, and I fell in love with the sisters. My friends and I would stay after school and help do whatever we could. It seemed like we hardly ever went home. We wanted to be with the sisters. It was so much fun. There were three young sisters here at that time who were such an inspiration to me. It seemed they could communicate without words. I could sense the bond between them, and I wanted to be a part of that. They simply remembered me as a dumb kid who didn't say anything. I was so bashful. My attraction to the sisters wasn't the teaching; it was to become part of the group and the community. I told my father of my interest and he approved. In the fall of 1934, the sisters allowed me to go to their academy, a four-year girls' high school, and my father paid whatever he could. In my senior year I became a postulant, and right after graduation I joined the novitiate. I was eighteen years old. It was 1939. I was a junior for three years and made my final vows in 1942.

I began teaching grade school for about four years, but I was always destined to be a piano teacher. I slowly worked my way through my degrees, mainly taking correspondence credits and summer courses. I went to the University of North Dakota, as it was the university closest to us. After taking the maximum amount of correspondence credits, I then started taking summer classes. After many years, I guess it was from about 1939 to 1960, I finally received my bachelor's degree. I was then assigned to teach music at a school near the university, and my next degree went much faster; in only two years I received my master's degree in music. My friends at the University of North Dakota then arranged an assistantship for me at the University of Iowa where I could work on my doctorate. After working on the degree for two years I was called home for an election at the monastery, and to my surprise I was elected prioress. I had not yet taken my comprehensives or written my dissertation for my degree, but I was called to spend the next ten years serving the monastery as prioress. These were the years from 1967 to 1977. It was a time of many changes. Any successes I had at this time I attribute completely to the gift of the Holy Spirit, which comes with the office of the prioress. It was a time of possible polarization in monastic communities. There were those who wanted to forge ahead with the changes and those who wanted to be very conservative and wanted to keep all the old ways. Some communities actually split and formed two groups. It was my job, through the Holy Spirit, to try to moderate both sides and make the changes that the pope was telling us were needed through Vatican II. At the end of my ten years, we elected my successor with a nearly unanimous vote. The community maintained a remarkable degree of unity through very complex times. We had many people helping us, including psychologists who counseled some sisters who had difficulty with the changes and new freedoms that we had. As prioress I was also caught up in a controversy at the time between the town's doctors, whose support was split between our medical facility and another one in town. It was a very strenuous job for me, as I didn't know the hospital business, and I had to learn it fast. I was on a total of five hospital boards and our retirement home board—meetings, meetings, meetings. We gradually moved out of the hospital business. I felt like I was always wearing two or three hats, which is difficult for me, as I have a one-track mind. I also restructured all six books of our liturgy during my time as prioress.

When I look back on all the reforms of those years, I ask myself if we went too far. Did we give people too much independence? Have we lost our real sense of community? We do have a good community spirit here, but I worry if some of us are doing their own thing too much. During the times of change it was very difficult to see some sisters depart from the monastery; they, too, found it very painful to leave. It has also been hard to watch the diminishment of the community in numbers, strength, and energy as we grow older, and not many young people are joining us.

After my time as prioress I took a sabbatical and mainly just rested and tried to get back to the moderation of my monastic roots. I was a bit drained. To my amazement my mentor back at the University of Iowa said that I could come back, take my comprehensives, write my dissertation, and finish my doctorate even though fourteen years had passed since my two years there. So I did go back and spent two more years. I passed my comprehensives and began work on my dissertation, which was on the English Monastic Office in North America. Nearly all monasteries changed to the vernacular after Vatican II, and in 1967 monastic communities had the option to design their own Office, which led to many variations. I traveled to ninety-six monasteries and interviewed their choirmasters, musicians, composers, and attended their Office, and wrote about their history. In 1985, I finished the dissertation and received my doctorate and more or less retired. Every fall now I teach in the Elderhostel program at the

University of Minnesota, and I also have about thirty piano students. I have been over sixty years in this community.

❁

As I reflect on my many years here, I cannot say that I have no regrets at all. When I was a young sister I can remember finding it hard at times not having a family and husband. It has always been that the girl who would make the best wife and mother would also make the best nun — selflessness is the key to both. But the regret of not having one's own family is offset by so many other things gained in this way of life.

I also think back to the times when I had authority. I have regrets that I might have used that authority better. I hope I never hurt anyone with that authority. I certainly never did so intentionally.

Those regrets are more than offset by the joy this life has given me, the joy of teaching and seeing my students blossom. As a music teacher it is joyful to see the satisfaction and delight students have when they discover they can create something beautiful.

A joy I remember from my younger days was, after having been out on assignment for some time, coming home to the community in the summer. Seeing the sisters and even just the walls and the floors of the monastery was such a joy. Now when I see the younger sisters come back in the summer it is the same kind of joy.

Even our funerals are joyful. And even if the deceased sister might have been a bit hard to live with, someone will find something wonderful to remember about her. We sing triumphant songs, and it makes you feel it's worthwhile to die.

There is also joy in the work we do with the outside world. We are now doing more outreach into the local community to help poor people and those in need. Instead of focusing on schools and hospital work as we did in the past, we now focus on community work. This comes directly from our monastic life and the respect we have for others and the desire to share what we have.

As a music teacher I have always gone outside the monastery. I've always had more non-Catholic students than Catholics. Meeting these kids, loving them, and proving that I was not going to try to convert them has been an ongoing part of my contact with the outside world.

Our community has always been apostolic. We have worked with schools, hospitals, and other concerns. The problem was that the bishops were forcing us to be apostolic rather than monastic, so much so that we had a hard time trying to figure out what it was to be monastic. It has only been since the 1970s that we have tried to grapple with that word — "monastic." We now see our main work as being monastic — living the monastic life. I remember my junior-mistress as a very wise woman. She used to say that we were both apostolic and monastic — and that is much harder to be than one or the other. I've never forgotten that. We are still doing both, but now we are focused more on the monastic.

Another aspect of my relationship with the outside world was my education. All my higher education took place at secular schools; none was at what might have been the more protective environment of a Catholic college. I loved the University of North Dakota. They accepted me with the full habit, and I had many friends. The University of Iowa was also very accepting of me in my full habit. I got along very well, and once people got to know me they didn't care what I was wearing. I was invited to parties and had many interesting experiences. When I went back to finish my doctorate I didn't have the habit, and that didn't seem to make a difference either. My time in secular universities broadened me beyond what I might have experienced at a school where I had been living with other sisters.

A problem I see in the outside world is the neglect of community. Even families don't seem to have a true sense of community. It seems that individualism is creeping into families. Families need to eat together, worship together, laugh and cry together. Churches are trying to promote this, and it is a Benedictine value that can certainly benefit all.

I would hope people could see the value of monastic celibacy as a way of life. So many people have the misunderstanding that if you are women living with women or men living with men that you are homosexuals. I would hope people could understand that there is another kind of love besides conjugal love. There is a true celibate love we experience as monastics which frees us for so many kinds of love. I wish we could give the public an understanding of the positive aspects of what a truly celibate life means. I think it could help counter some of the overemphasis placed on sex in our society.

The Benedictine tradition is moderation in everything, including prayer. Benedict's outline for the common prayer based on Scripture is our foundation. This common prayer combined with *lectio divina,* prayerful reading, is the basis of our spiritual lives. In our common prayer the Psalms play a large role. They always have something to say to you. Happiness, sadness, suffering, and the full range of human emotions is expressed in the Psalms, and they help you through life.

Part of my spirituality is based on our vow of conversion. We are in a constant state of conversion and growth. But that includes the reality that you are not always wonderful and your shadow side comes through and is part of your spirituality as well. The shadow is needed to give some delineation to the rest of your life. So often experiences in our lives that seem so terrible at the time they happen, ten years later seem like the best thing that could have happened. This is what I mean by the shadow. If everything in your life is always smooth, you can make very little real progress. It's like you're just sliding. We need challenges and the opportunity for reflection.

In my younger days we had a lot of work to do, but that was balanced with our prayer life. We had a considerable amount of physical work to do—gardening, teaching, and housework all kept us busy—but no excess in anything. We had good, healthy food, we went to bed early and got up early. In our lives today some things are not as balanced as they used to be. Some of us work too much. Some of us eat too much. Some of us don't get enough exercise. Some of us stay up too late. That is not Benedict's way. I know we still strive for balance.

There are many parts of the Rule I find very meaningful. There are so many practical aspects of the Rule. Clothing should fit the individual and penance should also fit the deed and not be immoderate.

Benedict teaches reverence for all things. We are to treat our pots and pans as if they were vessels of the altar. We have a reverence for the earth. We have reverence for all people. I believe this means reverence for yourself, too. If you have reverence and respect for your body, you are not going to abuse it. This returns us to living the balanced lifestyle of the Rule. And to the first word of the Rule—"Listen!" You need to listen to the spirit within you. You need that spirit to grow. I also find significant the chapters on the arranging of prayer, the Liturgy of the Hours. Benedict sets down so many things on the reverence of prayer, but also says that if you don't like the way he arranges the Psalms you should set them up yourself. It is in this area of the Rule that Benedict establishes common prayer as an integral part of a monk's life. Even when I was going to high school here, I was attracted to the Divine Office. In study hall we could hear the sisters chanting Vespers. It was so wonderful. I said to myself, *Someday I'm going to be doing that.* From my earliest years in community, the Office has always meant a great deal to me.

I think monasticism will continue. It is something the Lord wants in this world. The monastic way has been here for thousands of years. I believe that not only will it not perish, but there will be a resurgence. I certainly cannot predict the form. It will undoubtedly be a different expression than what we have now. Our way of life is needed as an example of community, love, and respect for all things.

Sister

JANE FRANCES BROCKMAN

1908–2000

Sister Jane Frances was a member of the Benedictine community at St. Scholastica Monastery in Fort Smith, Arkansas.

When Sister Jane Frances was led into the room that had been arranged for our meeting, I saw a small, frail, nearly blind woman. Little did I know that I was about to encounter one of the strongest individuals I have ever met. In spite of her condition, her every thought was concern for my comfort and needs. She had entered the monastery at the age of thirteen; at the time of my visit she had spent seventy-seven years as a member. I soon learned of her remarkable career in teaching and administration, but because of her typical Benedictine humility I was not learning everything. Then, during one of our breaks, with the tape recorder off, she began talking about a friend of hers with whom she had led a fast to persuade the local bishop to allow black girls to be admitted to their parochial high school. This was in the early 1950s, and it may have been one of the first cases of integration in Arkansas.

Even though I spent only two or three short days with Sister Jane Frances, I felt a very strong emotional tie develop. If I had lived closer to her, I have no doubt I would have made frequent visits just to be in her presence.

A year after my visit, I received the news that Sister Jane Frances had suffered a serious stroke; the next year brought the news of her death. It may not make sense to experience such deep grief and sorrow over the illness and death of someone with whom you have spent only a handful of days, but I did. This became one of the fundamental lessons the Benedictines have taught me: Life is never steady. With good times you will have bad times; with love you will have sorrow. And vice versa.

Sister Jane Frances

AT THE END of the nineteenth century and the beginning of the twentieth century, there were waves of immigrants coming to this country from Europe. A wave that came after the Civil War was agriculturally inclined, and they looked for cheap land on which to begin their new lives. Many of these immigrants came up the Mississippi River and got off in Missouri and moved into the interior of the country from there. That is where my ancestors came from and the ancestors of many of our sisters here at St. Scholastica. We are primarily German, but we have a sprinkling of other nationalities as well. Many of the immigrants were Catholics and looked to settle somewhere where there was a priest and a Catholic church or would be soon. After time, in conjunction with these churches, small schools were established, usually run by sisters. These parishes became the centers of Catholic life in what were many times "unfriendly" Protestant areas.

These people were pioneers. They led a rugged, hard life. It was in such a community that I grew up. My parents were the second generation of these people. The first generation had lived in Nebraska, but my parents moved to north Texas. I would guess 60 to 70 percent of our sisters have about the same story. In these Catholic parishes there were usually two sisters teaching first through eighth grades. There was no high school. Life was very difficult, but we didn't really realize that. It was just the way things were, and we were satisfied. We were twenty miles from the nearest doctor and had no real medical care available to us.

We went through the sisters' school, and when we finished the eighth grade there was nowhere else to go. That is when many of us young girls decided to go to the convent. There was no question of where I would go to the convent. The sisters who were my teachers were the only sisters I knew. I liked my teachers and knew that I could become a teacher by joining their convent, St. Scholastica, as the primary mission of the convent was to send teachers to small communities. I was thirteen when I entered. I stayed as a postulant for two years and then novitiate for one year, and in those three years I finished my high school studies.

I began teaching grade school when I was eighteen. The older sisters taught the younger ones who were starting to teach. I don't think I did much harm. My main problem was that I was too nice to the kids in the beginning. I had third-, fourth-, and fifth-graders, and they were all Italians. Some of those fifth-grade boys were pretty big and they got out of hand. But I learned as I went along. I remember reading in a book on tips for teachers, "Remember, don't smile until Christmas." So I started out being strict the next year and established good discipline. I grew to greatly enjoy teaching. I taught grade school for about five years and then taught seventh and eighth grades at St. Joseph's Orphanage in North Little Rock for five more years. I thoroughly enjoyed those grades as well.

I was then sent to study for one year at Atchison, Kansas, and two years at St. Mary's at Notre Dame, where I received my bachelor's degree in math with a minor in Latin. I was then sent to Catholic University in Washington, D.C., where I received a master's degree in math.

I then returned to St. Scholastica where we had an academy, a high school for girls. I was appointed principal of the academy and I taught as well. I was just over thirty years old at the time, but I guess I had already had quite a bit of experience. In the late 1940s, we began to discuss the possibility of admitting black girls to our academy. Arkansas law said we couldn't permit them in our school, and our bishop would not allow us to let them enter. Some of us decided to fast one day a week until the bishop relented. He finally did, but we could only allow the black girls to come for classes, but not social events. In the fall of 1952, we enrolled two black girls, becoming what may have been the first integrated school in Arkansas.

After seven years as principal, I was elected prioress. At thirty-eight, I was a bit young for that. I served three four-year terms in succession, then I refused another, but was elected four years later for another term. After I finished my term as prioress, I was elected president of the Federation of St. Gertrude for six years. Then I returned to St. Joseph's Orphanage as the administrator, which I did for eight years. I then went to our retreat center, House of Prayer at Shoal Creek, and helped administer that until 1994, when my failing eyesight made it too difficult.

All the years spent in administration, I was doing what God called me to do, but what I really wanted to do was to teach. I was a good teacher, and I loved teaching and felt that administration was not my gift.

I've been back here at the monastery for the past four years where I'm focusing on my prayer life. It is pleasant here. Everyone is so helpful and well cared for. We have a wonderful infirmary. The community provides for us in every way.

I have no regrets in choosing a monastic life, not any permanent ones anyway — a few brief ones — a moment or two when I felt like I was going to explode. But seriously, I have never had a regret that led me to want to leave the community.

One of the happiest days of my life was the day we began singing the Divine Office in English. It was actually before the liturgical reforms of Vatican II. We were the first monastic community in the country who prayed the Office in the vernacular. We had received special permission from Rome to do this. It was a great encouragement for the whole community. It brought those sisters who did not know Latin into a greater understanding and appreciation of the Office. It was the beginning of many other changes that were to come with Vatican II. I love the liturgy. The work that we have done to develop our liturgy here at the monastery has given me much joy.

Vatican II was also connected to what gave me my most sorrow: the time a few years after Vatican II when what we call the exodus took place. Many young people left us in a very short time. It was a heartbreaking time. We had grown too rapidly. We had over three hundred sisters, and they didn't have adequate training in theology and philosophy. It was during the time when I was president of the Federation, and all the requests to leave from all seventeen communities in our Federation would come to me to send on to Rome.

I think the basic value is that all people are the work of God's hands. We are all God's creation. We have the obligation to regard others as such. There is no basis for racial prejudice or any other kind of prejudice — people who might differ from our culture or accomplishments. There may be people who have smaller ambitions or expectations than we have or are not interested in the same things we are. We need to have respect for all people. They, too, are God's work.

I think we need to work for fairness for all people in the economic sector. There needs to be education available for all. There needs to be equal pay for equal work. There needs to be gender equality in both the marketplace and church. Our community here is very strong on working for that gender equality in the church. We have made real progress on that in our monastic community. For example, when we have a funeral for one of our sisters, in the past it was always a priest who would bless the departed, but now our prioress does that blessing.

I think the outside world is sometimes better than we give it credit for. Certainly there is materialism and indifference to pain and suffering of others. You see it so much in big business, where two companies will merge and thousands of people will be laid off. But, on the other hand, there is also so much good in the outside world. There are many people working to help those who are needy or disadvantaged or the working poor. There are people and organizations out there trying to help people better themselves. I'm impressed with the work that many people are doing in the outside world.

We need to be involved to whatever extent we can in what goes on in the outside world. It's important that we don't come into the monastery and close the door behind us with the attitude that we'll just stay here and mind our own business. What is happening out there is relevant to us. We have to be alert to social and political issues and use whatever influence we have to try to improve things.

❁

The Benedictine tradition is the gospel structured for people who want to live in monasteries. The Rule interprets the gospel for the monastic in a direct and simple way. There is nothing extraordinary required of monastics other than that they leave their homes and come together in a community life. It's a life of regularity and dedication, leading to a continual growth in the spiritual life following the precepts of the gospel. The monastic life doesn't require us to be great mystics or miracle workers. It simply requires that we be faithful to God's call, to listen to him, and to respond to him. I love the Prologue of the Rule of St. Benedict. It is poetic, profound, broad, and gentle in its appeal. It's such a kindhearted call to listen and hear God.

I'm impressed with Chapter 3, "Summoning the Brothers for Council." St. Benedict says that when there is an important decision to be made, then all the brothers should be called to council — all of them, even the youngest — and all of them should be listened to. This was very contrary to practices in the sixth century. Some of Benedict's monks had been slaves before coming into the monastery. He said they all needed to be listened to because the Holy Spirit sometimes reveals to the youngest what is best. It's a real reminder to us always to listen and not get to the point where we think we know it all. It was radical then and it is now. The monks were obligated to speak up if they had something to say. Today some might hang back for fear of being appointed to a committee!

Chapter 58 is one that I like to read time and time again. It regards the admission of new members and the standards by which we are to judge them and decide on their entry to the community. In our case, the discernment process takes some time. The primary consideration is whether they are here to truly seek God. Next, are they dutiful to the work of

God, which is the Divine Office? Are they here for a life of obedience and humility? Those are the standards by which we are to judge people wishing to join us. The first question is surely the most important of all. I still ask that question myself very often. Do I truly seek God? That is the most important thing in my life. I can look at that as my standard and see how I am doing by the kind of decisions I am making and how my prayer life is going. Keeping this question in my mind is a great help in coming closer to God, which is why I'm living this life.

Prayer is the very foundation of our spirituality. Time is allotted for all members to pray together. According to Benedict, we follow the *opus Dei* — the work of God, which is prayer. The Psalms make up the bulk of our community prayer life. Personally we have our *lectio,* our private spiritual reading and reflection.

In my many years of teaching, we were busy with the children all day but we prayed the Divine Office together in the morning and evening. Certainly our spiritual life suffered some, for there is only so much you can do. Every evening we had to get ready for the next day, and each teacher had two or three grades she was teaching. There was a deep devotion to teaching and the children — to do your best to help and enlighten them. Our life was really too busy for much spiritual growth, but we were spending our time on good work and the Lord provided for us spiritually somehow.

There is a deep regularity that comes into your life in a monastic community. You have your meals at the same time every day, prayer at the same time throughout the day, regular hours of retiring and rising. This kind of regularity is good for your health. It is a rhythm that preserves you from a great deal of anxiety. There is not a worry if you can get the rent paid or how you will pay your dental bills and so on. Many burdens are lifted from you.

There is also something in the Benedictine tradition about a closeness to the earth. Many of us here in this community were from farming backgrounds. We learn here that the earth is a good place. We have gardens and flowers. We like to cultivate the earth and be close to it. It's been said that if you go into a toolshed and all the tools are clean and properly ordered, you know you are probably in a Benedictine monastery. In recent years we have been very active in promoting the care of the earth. We have a true concern for the earth as we realize our oneness with it.

I'm an optimist — maybe an optimist gone to seed. I think back to our mother community in Eichstätt in Germany. The very first Benedictine sisters that came to America came from Eichstätt. The sisters have been in the same place in Germany for a thousand years. They have gone through many phases, from prosperity to nearly being wiped out. But when it looked hopeless for them, they never lost hope. They kept their membership between fifty and one hundred sisters and sent out missions when their membership increased. They are still a healthy community. They don't aspire to great numbers.

I think this is also what our community will do. We will grow smaller, maybe down to forty or fifty sisters. It's inevitable. We have many elderly sisters, but we also have new members joining us. Just one or two joining a year makes a big difference in the long run. I think as we grow smaller, we will become more monastic. We will be able to educate our sisters to a very high level of spirituality. While we were known in our first one hundred years as an institution that staffed the parochial schools, in the second one hundred years I hope we will become known as a center for spiritual resources for laypeople. I think we can be very effective as monastic models and teachers for spiritual direction. There is much we can do in providing for the spiritual growth of laypeople.

Father

CLEMENT PANGRATZ

Born 1919

Father Clement is a member of the Benedictine community at St. Martin's Abbey in Lacey, Washington.

❂

Sammy and I arrive at St. Martin's in the late afternoon. We settle into our room and share the evening meal with the monks. I think it would be best to start the meeting the next morning, but Father Clement is ready and fired up to get going after evening prayer. We talk until I am exhausted and have to go to bed. Father Clement recommends we start the morning with a walk through their beautiful wooded grounds. I agree and anticipate a short walk with the octogenarian. We walk at quite a brisk pace until, once again, I am exhausted. Later in the afternoon when I have recuperated, I experience one of the most poignant moments of this book's entire creation: I ask Father Clement what has given him the most sorrow in his life. He tells me how at the age of twelve he heard the doctor in the next room tell his parents that his father would soon die of cancer. He speaks of his great sorrow and the poverty of his family after his father's death. He tells me how he had gotten a job at a dairy doing maintenance, getting up at 3:30 a.m. and working until it was time to go to school. He earned $2.50 a week, money to help support the family. His thoughts then go to his mother and family. His eyes dampen and he says to me, "But I was fortunate. My childhood was really great." It is said with the deepest sincerity. At that moment I know that not only am I speaking with a wonderful person, but someone who represents a time that seems long, long past — a time when a child would rise in the middle of the night and work gladly to help support a family that gave the child so much love that material hardship was negated or minimized by the depth of affection.

Father Clement

I'M FROM Port Angeles up in the Washington coastal straits. It is a place that seems to have always been Benedictine. Our priests came from here, St. Martin's. I was raised in the Catholic school run by the Sisters of St. Anne. Father Bernard was the core of the church back in the 1920s and 1930s in that area. We lived in an isolated spot in the very northwest corner of the country. I went to daily Mass, and one day Father Bernard told me he thought I should become a priest. My older brother, John, was planning on joining but was killed in a hunting accident. I didn't think too much about Father Bernard's suggestion, but I did promise to see the abbot who was visiting in a few weeks. I put on my suit and went down to see the abbot when he came. He looked at me for a long time in silence. Then he said, "So, you want to be a priest?" Well, it was the first time that question had been put directly to me. I thought about it a while and said, "Yes." It was a wonderful blessing. He made the arrangements and I came to St. Martin's in 1938. It was wonderful. I remember I wrote in my papers, "Nothing will stand in the way of my becoming a priest unless God's will lets me know otherwise."

Looking back at it, it was pretty good for a nineteen-year-old kid. The opportunity here was a thrill. I loved it, and I still love it. The outdoors was tremendous. I would spend time by myself in the mountains. The rivers at that time were teeming with fish. Game was abundant. I was even yodeling up there. Academically I was not very well prepared. I didn't take the right courses in high school because I had no idea I was headed here. I had to work hard, but I had the determination. Latin was difficult, but I had said nothing would stop me. Four of us entered that year and all four of us persevered. I studied two years and then entered as a novice. We had a wonderful novice master, and Abbot Lambert was so upbeat. He also brought our college up to a four-year institution. I had learned the piano at the insistence of my mother when I was in grade school. Here I started learning to accompany Gregorian chant on the organ. I went to Mount Angel Seminary in Oregon to study theology and graduated in 1947. I learned a bit more about the organ at Mount Angel as well. After I was ordained, I took a year and a half correspondence from the Gregorian Institute, followed by a six-week seminar as review. There I was introduced to a new publication on the eighteen principles of Gregorian accompaniment. From these experiences I learned to be an accompanist for our liturgical services. I was very fortunate to have those experiences. For quite a number of years, I taught music at St. Martin's College. It was providential. Things happened, and I did the best I could.

Working with religious personnel has been my main work. I assisted the novice master in dealing with the novices. Pre–Vatican II they did not associate with the entire congregation as they do now. I was also brother master for a time, again personnel work. We worked on all kinds of projects: gardening, farming, sawmill work, running heavy equipment, and maintenance. I still do a great deal of outdoor work. I like to see what needs to be done and do it. Work and prayer are big with me. My mother was a great worker. We were nearly self-sufficient when I was a child. I also do considerable pastoral work. On the weekends I have worked the military bases, V.A. hospital, state mental institution, hospitals. I also did parish work from 1965 to 1981. I was sent to do parish work in

Alaska three times. I was always in an assistant position in my parish work, which was all right with me.

Now, I am helping out at Sacred Heart parish. I visit three nursing homes and say Mass once a month. Every Saturday at the retirement community, Panorama City, I preach and say Mass. I still do considerable studying for my assignments. Every night I spend in my room reading. I feel at home outside the monastery. I was never lonesome when I was doing pastoral work. I was sent, and I tried to live the monastic values. I didn't get into trouble. I loved the people and was edified by them. They were always so accepting of me. The remote missions were always so appreciative. I always felt it very easy to fit back into the monastic community when I returned from pastoral work. I have a deep sense of loyalty to St. Martin's. The values here are the same we had at home when I grew up.

Conversion as seeking God in the whole self is a tremendous value. It is a spiritual pursuit of becoming more Christlike. Stability is another great value — the stability of belonging. A monk's day is all related to religion. It becomes as the air you breathe. I love to balance my reading studies with nature. The abbot and I and several others are bird watchers. We get so much enjoyment from that. Peace and stability are so important. Benedict doesn't want us to worry. Peace can be lost both by worrying and by wanting. I love to look out of my window both day and night and enjoy the scene — appreciating God's creation. My years in music have helped me develop some sensitivity.

I feel a joy in the life I'm living. It's creative in my spiritual life. I can study and keep learning all the time. I can share it, and that's a joy. There is a rhythm to our lives day in and day out over the years that produces a quiet, simple joy. But it's not a utopian thing. We do have tensions and problems. Buildings, money, closures, staff, and other things can cause traumas. That's life. We have to adjust and adapt. Everything can't be controlled.

I feel I am a part of the Benedictine tradition here at St. Martin's. I try to live it and understand the historical traditions that go back to St. Benedict. I love our daily schedule of prayer. The music involved means a great deal to me. We sing much of our prayer. The Divine Office must be done with much care and reverence. My spiritual reading of modern authors complements my prayer life and gives me assurance and contentment. I try to learn more and more about the mysteries of my faith. The liturgy, of course, is the supreme source of all my prayer and inspiration. Our prayer is personal responsibility to account to God for all the gifts he has given us. I'm realizing this more all the time.

The tradition creates a framework for practicing charity with others. St. Benedict tells us that if you have an argument with a member of the community, you are to go to them and settle it before the sun goes down. Well, I've never had that experience in my many, many years here. Isn't that strange? I've never thought about it before, but I've never had to do that. I've had difficult times over the years, but the determination with grace that I started with as a nineteen-year-old has helped me. No one has ever pushed me around, and I've always come through it. I've never held malice toward anyone and always looked for an opportunity to become close to a person with whom there may have been temporary tensions. Well, it works.

Now that I'm up in years, some people see me as a bit of a character. That's half the battle; they don't take me too seriously. We get along very well. You have to earn respect. Not self-respect; that can be selfish. It is not what you say but what you are. When they can kid you for what you are without malice, it's a kind of well-meaning respect. We have an abundance of freedom, but that freedom must be used properly or others will suffer. Freedom is a responsibility; all suffer if one misuses it. Charity is the supreme virtue. All others are included in it. Sometimes it's easy; sometimes it's hard.

The emphasis on the worship is very special to me. The order and structure in the Rule are wonderful. In the old days, everything was to be provided within the enclosure of the monastery. The mill, the garden, the water, the trades, the church, everything was to be self-contained. It was quite a system, a fine example to the warring society of that time. The Rule also sets forward a very good administrative system of personnel. It has order and moderation. All the structure is for one purpose — to seek God.

There have been some hard times, even times when we were worried we might have to move, but I haven't heard anything like that for some time. The college is doing very well. It has good enrollment, an excellent reputation, and great teaching. We have the wisdom of our Confederation of Abbeys who meet with the abbots and committees once a year and discuss and plan to adapt as needed while maintaining the spirit of the Rule.

I cannot imagine any other life that I would rather live than my life as a monastic. I thank God that I came to St. Martin's. We have a special spirit here. I love it here. Our superiors have insisted on charity to one another, and it has been so. I feel that God put me here.

Sister

M. MATTHIAS IGOE

Born 1923

Sister Matthias is a member of the Benedictine community at San Benito Monastery in Dayton, Wyoming.

San Benito is a unique monastery among the ones I am visiting. It is a community of just five sisters, whose mother monastery is Sisters of Perpetual Adoration in Clyde, Missouri. The modified family home has a lovely setting at the foot of the Big Horn Mountains. A stream from the mountains runs by the house and provides a wonderful background sound for the Divine Office. Wild turkeys roam the grounds, trees are full with blossoms, and robins chirp. Visitors are greeted by the warm family atmosphere of the sisters. The twenty minutes of silent prayer before Divine Office make me feel especially at home, since I meditate half an hour every day. My conversation with Sister Matthias is fluid and heartfelt. When I ask her if she has any regrets for having chosen a monastic life, I receive an unexpected answer: "Every woman regrets not having a child. I had to decide when I joined the community if I was running away from the responsibility of motherhood and marriage. I saw that I was not running away; rather I saw another way of loving, caring, and giving. At the same time I see something very beautiful in the spousal relationship and the relationship of child and mother. This does create a void, but it is not that my life must have every void filled — that is not the human condition. If everything were filled I would be God. This is one of the voids in my life, a void which gives me a way of experiencing God in a special way." The honesty, depth, and sincerity of her response stuns me. The forfeiture of marriage and children is an aspect of monastic life that many laypeople find difficult to grasp. This frank explanation is an insight that helps me have a greater understanding of the celibate life.

Sister Matthias

I GREW UP in St. Louis, Missouri, and was the middle one of three sisters. My father was of Irish descent and my mother of German descent. We grew up in a lower-middle-class neighborhood. At that time, St. Louis was called the Rome of the West due to the dominance of Roman Catholics. A large part of my early history was being part of our parish. It was a small parish of about 250 families, but it had a farsighted pastor who set up not only a school but also a community center that was the hub for everyone in the parish. We always lived within three blocks of the church and center, so we were continually in and out. It was a constant part of our lives. When you entered the sixth grade, you automatically became part of the choir. You didn't question the system; you went with the flow. I went to the Catholic high school and rode the streetcar back and forth. My parents wanted us to have a Catholic education, and to make that possible my mom got a job at a shoe factory. Even through the Depression, Dad was never unemployed; he always managed to make enough to keep us going. But in the hard times there was a sense of closeness in the whole neighborhood. People helped one another out. The high school I attended intentionally did not make it a social center as well. They wanted you to focus your social life on the parish, not the school. I grew up with a close sense of community focused on the parish.

My personality was quite introverted. I loved books. Sometimes during summer vacation I would read up to three books a day. At the same time I did like sports and would play basketball with my friends. I enjoyed a quiet, speculative life. I loved to lie out on the grass and look up at the clouds, imagining animals and figures. I had skipped two grades in grade school and I graduated from high school at sixteen. I was then fortunate to receive a scholarship to Fontbonne College in St. Louis. It was run by the Sisters of St. Joseph as an institution for women associated with St. Louis University, which was all male at that time. Even then I thought I would like to be a sister, but I knew I was too young and needed to develop more. I majored in sociology and went on for a master's degree in social work. Then I worked at Catholic charities for a couple of years and thoroughly enjoyed my work. I kept thinking about joining the sisterhood, but something kept getting in the way. At one point I was about to get serious about entering when my mother needed surgery and she told me that my younger sister had decided to enter the Sisters of St. Joseph. So I saw it as an indication that God wanted me to stay home and be with Mother.

About two years later, I felt the call again and began looking at communities. It was important for me to know I had the qualities to be a good wife and mother and was not running away from this responsibility. I reached a point in my life where I wished to give myself totally to a search for God. The spiritual director of my parish helped me search for communities and to learn more about them. I was nearly twenty-eight at this time. My family supported my decision. When I visited the Benedictine Sisters of Perpetual Adoration in Clyde, Missouri, everything resonated. I had a special affinity with the Eucharist, and their devotion to the Eucharist was very appealing. It was also a community that — while being very supportive — was also challenging. The sisters were full of kindness and cheerfulness.

There were also signs on my first visit. My watch stopped on my arrival and did not work while I was there (it then continued to work perfectly for the next ten years). On the last day of my visit they served my favorite dessert, banana cream pie, which they had not served for years. I went home and prayed over my decision. Using my sociology background, I also did a discernment chart on all the communities I had visited, looking at my strengths and weaknesses, and those of the communities as I perceived them. The best match came out to be Clyde. This helped me to give myself totally to my decision in the beginning. There were some things I didn't like back in the 1950s, but I understood they were part of the package and I was willing to accept them. Some of the spirituality back then was not very healthy, and having the psychology training that I did, I knew it was not healthy. I had to learn how to give myself to the healthy side and not get caught up in the unhealthy side. I loved the community and I loved the sisters. I still do. I entered in 1951, made profession in 1953, and final vows in 1958.

As a novice they assigned me to the kitchen to "test my vocation." What they didn't realize was that I liked to cook and enjoyed the kitchen. After about seven months they thought they were promoting me to work in correspondence. What they didn't know this time was that I hated writing letters. We were handling a correspondence with forty-five thousand subscribers to our magazine, *Tabernacle and Purgatory,* at that time, so there was a great deal of letter writing. I did appreciate that writing letters was a service and grew to like it. People who wrote us needed a reply. After a couple of years I also was assigned to teach Latin to those coming into the order. I didn't know Latin other than the few years I had in high school. Now when I talk to some of the sisters who were in those classes, they just howl with laughter. Many of them had had five or six years of Latin before they came. I was later sent to St. Mary's at Notre Dame because our bishop had felt there was not enough theology being taught at our monastery. At that time the degree was called a doctorate in sacred doctrine, as they couldn't award doctorates in theology to women in those days. I was there for two and a half years and then returned to Clyde and was assigned to be the secretary for the monastery. In 1965, I was sent to be the subprioress at our Kansas City priory. This was during the turmoil of Vatican II. Before Vatican II we did not read newspapers, we did not watch TV, and only a few magazines were read. But five of our sisters spent five summers at St. John's in Collegeville, Minnesota, studying and understanding the changes. There was so much change happening, and there was opposition to some of it. It was a time of unrest. Sisters were leaving, or thinking of leaving, the community. It was a period of considerable pain and heartache in losing dear friends. We attempted to renew ourselves, and we rewrote our constitution. I ended up being assigned as prioress at our Tucson monastery from 1968 to 1974. I really wanted to stay in Kansas City, but the prioress-general said I was to go to Tucson. I ended up loving it there. I served two terms as prioress, the maximum allowed by our constitution, then returned to correspondence in Clyde for a year and a half. I was then assigned to help execute a study plotting future needs of the congregation. For this I resided with our sisters in St. Louis and traveled to all our communities for workshops and discussions. After that, I returned to Clyde and participated in an experimental small group living inside the larger community. Five of us tried to create a smaller, simpler, communal life within the larger monastery. The situation did not fare well because there was too much adjustment required on both sides of the issue. We requested to relocate elsewhere or disband. As the

Chapter had approved the founding of the Osage monastery at this time, they did not deem it feasible to start a second new group. I was then elected to the General Council, where I remained for eight years in St. Louis, participating in the planning for the congregations. My parents, who were still in St. Louis, were in ill health, and I was allowed to help care for them for some years. Then I served as subprioress in St. Louis for three years.

A year and a half ago, I visited this community in Wyoming and joined. It is, again, a small community of five sisters. I am very much enjoying it here. In a large community I can get lost in my own world. I can go off and nobody really knows. A small community like this challenges you, and you are needed. I also find it easier to share my spirituality and inner feelings in a small group rather than with fifty people. The small group is not for everyone, but it should be a possibility for those who need it.

In my relationship with God and with others, I need to feel that I am significant and that I am significant for someone. It isn't the job you have but the relationship with the other members and with God that is important. Joy in my life has come through the relationships I have had with God and with people. That reaches from childhood to the present. My parents were not saints, but they were great people. I stayed home as long as I did because I wanted to know them as they were. I got to know them as friends as well as parents. I understood their fights, their frustrations, and their joys. My mother never tired of telling of her boyfriend who took her on dates on his motorcycle in 1918. I think my father got even by giving me the middle name of his previous girlfriend. I have received so many joys from the sisters I have been with and also the great joy of sitting quietly with the Lord — sitting and just being.

Conversely, my main sorrow that I carry is the knowledge that there have been times when I could have done things better than I did. I know I need to accept that and move out of it, yet there is sadness. This is especially true for times when I was in leadership and made bad decisions, certainly not deliberately, but one looks back and regrets. There was also the time of sorrow in the 1960s when people were leaving our monastic communities. It was a sad time of separation.

The monastic life has challenged me to see the outside not as a separate entity but also as a part of who I am. Before Vatican II, we could not go home to visit our families. They could come for three days of visit per year at the monastery. The wisdom of the group overcame that. The Benedictine life has given me a frame of reference in which I can work and relate. When I look back with a historical perspective at what today seem harsh regulations of the past, some are understandable. It was an overprotective attitude, but society at the time of the formulation of these rules was very rotten. It was their way of saying we care enough for you that we don't want these terrible things happening to you, so the safest thing is to lock you up. They didn't realize that the locking up was also violating the individual. I am a firm believer that no matter what is going on, there is always a ferment to raise us a little higher.

Because of my background and training in social work, my prayer has always included the poor and the lonely.

My foundation is the Eucharist and the Benedictine life. The key for Benedict is the Christ-orientation. Humility is the truth of God and the truth of the person I am. We are called to be one within that. You must always respect those you live with. You might not understand her or maybe even like her, but you respect those differences. The Eucharist has always been a special part of my life. From going to church with Mom and Dad, to my first communion at the age of six, I knew something was happening between God and myself. By the age of twelve, when I was in choir, the Eucharist became a true moment of union. I then went to daily Mass through high school and college. In my twenties I became the young sophisticate and only went to Sunday Mass for a while. But I kept coming back to the Eucharist as the point where God and I relate, as well as I and the world. It is love that inserts itself in all humankind.

My first years of community life were very ascetical. It was difficult and regimented. There were long hours of group prayer and work with little time for personal prayer. Now we have the capability to set up our schedules to meet our needs, especially in our small group. That doesn't mean we change things willy-nilly. We have anchor points to keep our stability. If I am having problems, I don't have to go to strangers. The community is always there to help in every way. We work for our living. We try to support ourselves. I am at the point in my life that the intellectual life is not what I am most interested in. I want to savor my experiences. I want to create things, even though the end product might not be so hot.

I have found that Chapter 7 of the Rule of Benedict on humility is the core. We must live in the presence of God. For me that is being who you are and who he has called you to be and who he has given you the potential to be. The call is to listen and respond and allow yourself to grow. That includes mistakes, failings, challenges, and delights — embracing the full human condition in the light that God created. As I am a person created in God's likeness, my values have to be that I attempt to become like God — that is, to pursue love, mercy, and compassion. The perfection of God is that he is a God of love and a God of compassion. That is what I am called to be.

I am very hopeful for the future. I have been taught since childhood to enjoy life. Life always has its ups and downs, but it will go on and it will go on in different and new ways. I hope the community continues to choose those things that will make it alive. San Benito is a vision of change and living together. We must continue to change as Wyoming changes and support the community with our adaptation.

Father

VINCENT MARTIN

1912–1999

Father Vincent was a member of the Benedictine community at St. Andrew's Abbey in Valyermo, California.

The resortlike layout of St. Andrew's in the San Gabriel Mountains north of Los Angeles makes it a truly exotic place, with Joshua trees dotting the landscape and small lizards darting from rock to rock. Sammy and I stayed in a small cabin perched on a hillside overlooking the monastery. In the night the rustling of small creatures made me wonder what desert animals we might be sharing quarters with.

Father Vincent possessed a towering intellect. His first-rate education and global experience had sharpened his insight and made him a keen observer and critic of modern culture. His life seemed like rich material for the screenwriters in nearby Hollywood. I was in awe of the man, his exceptional life, and what he had contributed to both his community and ecumenical religious relations.

Father Vincent

I WAS NOT a very religious person. Growing up in southern Belgium I was a good Catholic, but very worldly in my tastes and activities. At the end of my high school years, I decided to make a retreat at a Jesuit house. There I had the experience of a personal conversion. I was still a precocious sixteen-year-old, but I did start to think about what I was going to do with myself. I went on to decide very quickly that I wanted to be a monk. I wanted to go to the root—to what is basic.

My father was a successful physician. He and my mother, who died when I was seven, traveled a great deal. The house was full of items from their travels, and my mother had a great stamp collection. They created in me an interest and opening to the larger world outside Belgium. I was also a student of the Jesuits, who emphasized their mission work. This led me to combine a deep desire to be a monk with an equal drive to be a missionary. These two goals did not seem to be compatible. I then discovered St. Andrew's Abbey in Belgium, known for its mission work in Africa and China. It answered my desire to be both a monk and a missionary. I received the name Vincent for the famous Father Vincent Lebbe, a Belgian missionary in China. He very much identified with their culture, was anticolonial, a great champion of acculturation. After I entered the monastery, I studied philosophy and theology. We were blessed with top-notch professors who were teaching in the 1930s the theology that would become the basis for Vatican II thirty years later. I was ordained in July of 1936, and by September of that year I was on my way to China.

When I arrived in China I spent several years learning the language. We were six monks in a small monastery in

Sichuan. In 1937, war in China began. Father Vincent Lebbe with a group of Christian volunteers joined the Chinese Army Medical Corps. I received permission to go and help him. I ended up as a lieutenant colonel in the Nationalist Chinese Army commanding a medical battalion of about three hundred volunteers. After two and a half years and eleven big battles, we were finally surrounded by the Japanese and taken prisoner. I was in various Japanese prison camps for over two years. After the end of World War II and my release, I wanted to return to Sichuan, but the U.S. Army kept me as a Chinese liaison officer to the American Marines for six months. It was some of the toughest work of my life. I was given the job of evacuating a Japanese hospital of two thousand Japanese soldiers dying of tuberculosis. I contracted the disease myself and had to be discharged from the army. After a short visit to Sichuan I returned to Belgium, visited my family, and then went for a stay in Switzerland to regain my health.

It was decided that I should go to Harvard University to qualify me to teach at a university in Sichuan. I started at the summer school at Harvard in 1948. When the communists in China began to threaten the monastery, I wanted to return, but my superior wouldn't let me return without my degree, so I remained at Harvard. The monks in China were expelled by the communists in 1951 and 1952. It was a very difficult time. I felt very Chinese, and I still do in my subconscious. I continued working on my doctorate in sociology at Harvard. It then became my job to find a new location for our community in the United States. I looked at about two hundred possible sites in the Los Angeles Diocese and eventually settled on this site at Valyermo. We started with three hundred acres and we now have more than six hundred acres and also a good well that yields four hundred gallons per minute, which is very important for our future in the desert.

In 1956, we began the regular monastic life at Valyermo. I was put in charge of the retreat center. We began organizing a fall festival that today draws twenty-five thousand people and at least six hundred volunteers to help us. In 1964, I spent a year at Weston Priory in Vermont as master of novices and then four years in Jerusalem at Dormition Abbey on Mount Zion. I learned Hebrew and did postgraduate work at Hebrew University.

I returned to Valyermo in 1969 and served as subprior, master of novices, and guestmaster. I had been a close friend of Thomas F. O'Dea, the well-known sociologist of religion in America. He died of cancer, and through our association I started teaching some of his courses at the University of California in Santa Barbara. Membership in the Ecumenical Commission of the Archdiocese of Los Angeles gave me the opportunity to become involved in the Christian/Jewish dialogue. I became very close to the Jewish community, and as Catholic chaplain at Cedars-Sinai Medical Center I helped the hospital to start a Jewish chaplaincy.

In 1986, I celebrated the fiftieth anniversary of my ordination to the priesthood. I was retired from my function as guestmaster and soon afterwards was invited by the director of the Tantur Ecumenical Research Institute in Jerusalem to serve as the director of worship. I was there for six years and researched a book on the parting of the ways between the synagogue and the church in the first century, entitled *A House Divided.*

After my return to Valyermo I served as subprior again. This is my home; I am a good Californian. But after ten years in China and ten years in Israel, I also feel very Chinese and very Israeli. It helped me to be Chinese with the Chinese. Benedictines tend to be rooted in the land and the community. Benedictines have a special relation to the Asian churches with these qualities. It is easy for a Buddhist or a Protestant to be comfortable with Benedictines. We go beyond the conflicts of dogma. We are better prepared for a dialogue with non-Catholics. In our work at the retreat house, we have fruitful relations with many non-Catholics.

Life has had joys and sorrows. I've been a kind of achiever, trying to achieve things and most of the time failing. Sometimes I succeeded, and it brought me moments of enjoyment. I have had some very nice friendships through the years. I have had human relationships that were not goal-oriented and were satisfying because of this quality. I experienced many moments of worship that were very joyful. Joy is a by-product and not something I look for. The search for happiness has no meaning. If you search for it, you will probably never be happy. I believe in building. My humanism and spirituality are to build the kingdom of God. You don't build the heavenly kingdom in heaven; you build it on earth. Birth is a long process. Society birth, cultural birth, is always a long process. What remains and what disappears forever is difficult to know. We are in the womb of nature like we were in the womb of our mother. Something is happening all the time until we are born, for better or for worse. You can be stillborn, or you can add to the splendor of creation. I have tried to lead a contemplative life, remaining aware that I am in a process of becoming. Often it made me responsive to a specific goal for a period of time. Happiness for me is when you function well in those capacities. Happiness is not the lack of challenge, but that things are going somewhere, even when it is hard, painful, and difficult, like a woman delivering a baby. It's not pleasant, but it's meaningful. The thing that is difficult is to have to do something that is meaningless.

While I have had few outstanding successes, I've also had few outstanding failures. Certainly the loss of my mother at the age of seven was a deep sorrow. I lost my father during the war and didn't know it for six months. I have lost many dear friends. These are all sorrows. On the other hand, I have a deep conviction that they are with God, and this is a source of happiness. I could have done many other things, but I am happy to have been in the Benedictine tradition. It seems to me significant. I don't think I could have done forty or fifty years of apostolic work in the world. I need the balance of the Benedictine way of life.

I have been very comfortable with the Benedictine tradition because of its moderation. It goes with my nature. As a young person I may have been a bit of an extremist at times, but as my life has gone on I have become middle-of-the-way. I'm a liberal on the Right, or a conservative on the Left. Living in community you have to find compromises. A hermit can go to extremes. The Benedictines go back to the undivided church of the early centuries. We still enjoy a true biblical spirituality. Look at the Divine Office. I feel very comfortable with this and my interest in biblical studies. I am open to change when that change is meaningful. We have been reformed so often. Our value for survival is to keep tradition alive. Reform can make things better, but you need to be careful not to overdo it. Creativity and tradition need to work together.

I very much enjoy community life. But circumstances have often taken me away from community. I have been able to do some pioneering work and been quite influential in many ways, but I have never been in a position of leadership. Things have never worked that way. My life has been shaped by circumstances.

In my early schooling I was influenced by the Jesuits, but I became very interested in the liturgical movement. This was reinforced when I joined the Benedictine monastery. As a young monk I was first attracted to the study of the church fathers. Slowly I became more involved in biblical studies. My stays in Israel greatly reinforced this interest. Now I always read the Bible in Hebrew. It is so much more alive. I believe biblical studies are the foundation and life of the church. They are the bases of any sound spirituality. The world of the Bible is so different from the world of today. It can be difficult.

We are living in a time that is more religious than it was fifty or sixty years ago. However, the biblical God is disappearing. People are open to the divine, but Yahweh is being ignored. There is a strong influence from India and a return to a kind of pantheism. We are seeing much concentration on the humanity of Christ, and with it the sense of the sacred is lost. People don't seem to be really worshipping. They get together and feel good—a kind of new opium for the people. It is a very serious problem. The sense of God, the sense of the transcendent, the sense of worship is failing.

Another great problem is a radical individualism that has gone way too far. The Catholic Church brought to America a wonderful concept: the common good. The parish and neighborhood caring was a strong asset. That too seems to be failing in today's America. Parishes have become service stations. They often don't go beyond friendship communities, which is important but not enough. We are living on borrowed spiritual capital from the past. We don't replenish it. We have a very strong economic system, a kind of economic feudal system. It is always working but will sacrifice the individual without a second thought. Profit is the only value; everything is sacrificed to profit. It taps a great deal of energy, but finally what kind of society are we going to have? Motivation today is motivation to succeed and make as much money as possible. It's hard to see how this society will function. I see our Benedictine communities as small islands of sanity in this confusion, much like St. Benedict's community was back in the sixth century.

I do have hope for the future. I have hopes for the church and our congregation. We have a new spring in the community right now. I hope it continues. We are a pluralistic monastery; we work in many directions. It may be a problem to maintain this pluralism, but it is also a strength.

Sister

JOEINE DARRINGTON

Born 1915

Sister Joeine is a member of the Benedictine community at Queen of Angels Monastery in Mount Angel, Oregon.

Queen of Angels Monastery suffered a major disaster a few years before our visit. An earthquake had caused major damage to many of the buildings. But in typical Benedictine spirit, the advanced years of many of the members did not stop them from an all-out effort to rebuild the monastery. As we arrive, Sammy and I receive a tour of the new living quarters for the sisters. With a sense of delight it is pointed out that each room now has its own sink — a luxury never dreamed of by many sisters. The grounds of the monastery are an explosion of color; flowers are everywhere. The well-groomed beds layer profusions of reds, yellows, and purples, bordered by a variety of rich greens. The elder chosen for my portrait is Sister Joeine, the self-professed "convent hugger." It is a well-deserved title as she has a heart as big as a room, but she most certainly has qualities that go beyond her loving nature; with sixty-two hours of credit beyond her doctorate degree, she also has a superb intellect.

Sister Joeine

THE PLAINS of central Montana were my home for ten years. We walked a mile and a half to the one-room school where I attended grades one through six. I loved both school and reading. The light from a kerosene lamp was a challenge, but it didn't discourage me from enjoying every storybook I could find.

We traveled twelve miles to church in a double buggy pulled by two horses. It took two hours to get there and two hours to get back. My mother was a convert to Catholicism, and the region in which we lived was everything but Catholic. My religious background was poor although we did study the Baltimore Catechism each week. I still remember, "We need sufficient reflection and full consent of the will!" What does that mean to a six-year-old?

Crop failures, drought, hail, and grasshoppers finally forced us to move to town in 1925. My father found work in a flour mill where he earned a living for our family until he retired. I loved school, had excellent teachers, studied hard, and graduated as valedictorian of the class of 1932. Because of the Depression, college was out of the question. A friend who was employed by the railroad gave me a free rail pass to go to Portland, Oregon, to visit my sister who was a nurse at St. Vincent Hospital. I ended up working in Portland for a year, doing housework for the typical Depression wages of five dollars a month with room and board. During that year, some of my sister's friends directed us to a small teacher training college in Mount Angel, which was owned by Benedictine sisters. My sister and I visited the campus, where we were warmly welcomed by the traditional Benedictine hospitality. I enrolled as a college freshman in 1933. The sisters made generous financial arrangements for my sister and myself to meet the tuition charges.

From the first day, my college life was a wonderful new experience. I felt so at home with the sisters, who were sincerely interested in the few resident students they had at that time. My religious background was so sketchy that I was lost in the college religion classes, but the teachers didn't give me a sense of being hopeless. The annual college retreat occurred in January of 1934. This was my first really close contact with Benedictines, and I was uncertain as to what it all meant. Our college rector, a Benedictine priest, guided me through the retreat, explained religious vocation, and encouraged me to consider seriously the possibility. Five months after coming to the college, I felt drawn to convent life but still had no real idea what was involved. The rector arranged an interview for me with the Mother Superior. It was a scary idea that became a pleasant experience as she greeted me with a warm smile and encouraging words. That started the acceptance process. I shared the news with my parents and soon received a letter back from my mom saying, "Well, land's sake, Sis, if that's what you want to do, it's just fine." I went home that summer of 1934 for a final visit. Of course, my friends thought I had gone crazy — getting locked up in a "nunnery" for the rest of my life! No one changed my mind. On August 6, I said good-bye to everyone and returned to Mount Angel. I don't remember ever doubting my decision. It seemed like a vision come into place. I was welcomed and accepted on August 10, and pronounced final vows six years later, in 1940.

My main work for forty-four years was teaching. I started with two years of normal school training, and with two years of experience I was able to get a lifetime elementary teaching certificate. I taught in our high school for twenty-four years and was also principal for the last eight years. In 1964, the high school closed because of financial problems, and I moved into teaching in our monastery's college. I worked with the education department and with student teachers in the public schools. I had also been working on graduate classes and received my doctorate from the University of Portland in 1968. I had a wonderful time supervising student teachers. I remember the day I was visiting a second-grade classroom and the teacher was laughing when I arrived. We sisters were still wearing the black habits in those days, and the teacher said one of the little boys had just said to her, "Hey, we had better clean this joint up; the flying nun is coming today!" I had taught several classes in the college prior to 1968. I worked in the college for nine years until funding for my job ended. By that time I was well known in the public school system and was hired by a nearby elementary school in 1971 to teach fourth grade. This was an easy transition for me, as several faculty members had been in my classes at Mount Angel College and seemed to be pleased to have me become "one of them." It became quite a joke that with a doctorate, I didn't know enough to teach fourth grade. I continued taking graduate classes during my years in the public school. By the time I finished teaching, I had sixty-two hours of credit beyond my doctorate — not the usual state of affairs in the elementary classroom!

In my years of teaching and preparing teachers, I hope that the Benedictine sense of commitment and dedication was a source of inspiration that was obvious to my students and associates. In my interactions with the outside world, I do have some concern regarding the lack of positive direction of so many people's lives, but I do have a sense of hope as well.

In 1982, I retired from teaching and moved into other work at the monastery. This was not easy and took some practice. I quickly found myself being consumed by small jobs followed by bigger ones, until I simply had to learn how to say no without guilt. This was not easy and took some practice. I was on a variety of committees, boards, and teams. Some years later, my main work was helping to raise funds to repair and rebuild our monastery that was damaged by the 1993 earthquake. It was a long, difficult task, but we were successful in reaching our goal. I also worked with alumna projects. Presently, I go to many funerals; I am a volunteer at a prison in Salem, where I have many friends; and in my spare time I also animal-and-house-sit for friends.

My Benedictine vocation has given me so much joy in my life; there is nothing more precious and special. It has given me peace and joy for sixty-five years. I have been blessed by two gifts that bring joy. First, I am a person who enjoys people. Second, I am able to close doors and move on. In my life I have had to change directions or jobs or focus. When those times came, I didn't get ulcers or lose sleep. I simply moved on. Each move has had many positive, happy results.

But I have had some sorrows in my life. The sudden death of my only brother was a deep sorrow. It was also a deep sorrow to lose many of my dear friends in the 1950s and 1960s when they left our community. The devastation from the earthquake in 1993 was a sobering loss that nevertheless has resulted in many unexpected blessings and surprises.

I'm very healthy and have inherited good genes! My mother was ninety-three when she died. She ate dinner at 5:30 and died at 7:00. You can't beat that! Our daily schedule at the monastery is well balanced and allows time for exercise. I am in a water aerobics class three times a week. We have excellent medical care. I know that if I become ill, I'll be cared for here, I will die here, and I will be buried here in our cemetery. I haven't picked out my plot yet, but it's just a block down the path. There is a tremendous sense of security in my physical life, as there is in my spiritual life. I pray daily for continued good health. Growing older brings a different perspective on what is important in my day-to-day life. I have fewer expectations for myself and ask others to respect this. So few things are truly important — the daily rhythm of prayer and work, the blessing of friends and relationships, the gift of physical and mental health. I consider these priorities.

Our prayer life is the foundation for our Benedictine spiritual life. We gather four times a day as a group for prayer, and we also are blessed by celebrating the Eucharist daily. In my private prayer life, my goal is to begin each day with an hour of prayer and meditation. St. Benedict's idea of small independent groups of people based on a family style of living is so important to me. Our vow of stability roots me forever here in this place with these sisters. This has brought such a sense of security and peace and joy. To share the same hopes, plans, and dreams gives me a wonderful feeling of belonging, knowing that my home will always be here.

In regard to the Rule of St. Benedict, Chapter 53 on the reception of guests has very special significance to me. I'm sometimes called the "convent hugger," as I frequently welcome visitors, strangers, or passers-by. I often read Chapter 36 on the care of the sick. At one time, when my room was near the infirmary, I spent considerable time with older sisters there. I remember visiting one sister who had this large-print Bible in her hands. She said to me, "Sister, I have just finished reading the whole Bible, the whole Bible!" Then with her beautiful smile she added, "But I don't remember a word I read." Chapter 6 on silence is really the foundation for our daily *lectio* and meditation. Chapter 72 on good zeal is very special to me. Its insights on caring for and loving the people I live with are the very heart of the Rule. But there is much more that has significance for me. The entire Rule is truly a masterpiece.

A dramatic change occurred in our monastery during the 1960s. I call it the "time of liberation." My first thirty-three years were a very different time compared to the years after Vatican II.

On August 16, 1966, we were called into one of the most important meetings of my convent life. Our superior announced that we could start experimenting with contemporary dress. Our black habits soon became attractive suits, skirts, and dresses. This change was optional, and difficult for some while easy for others, and unacceptable to those who chose to continue wearing the traditional habit. Another "drastic" announcement was that we would now make decisions for ourselves and assume responsibility as adults. That was a surprise and even a shock. We could now leave the monastery by just signing the check-out book. We could budget our own small personal allowance. We could accept invitations to dinners, concerts, and plays. We could visit relatives without a companion. How can I convey the sense of freedom, of excitement, of the "new life" that these changes brought?

The most important announcement for me was that now we could develop deep, personal friendships, forbidden for so many years. These were innovative, unheard-of changes that our superior believed in. She saw them as implementing the guidelines of Vatican II. Those were truly wonderful days, and the changes have continued to be special parts of my day-to-day life.

Many people have developed false values that they attempt to impose on others: the value of material things, the value of money, the value of prestige, the value of social class, the value of high standards of living. People are missing what is so basic and important, even the value of permanence. People are moving around, changing jobs, changing marriages. Permanence seems to frighten people. Religion and prayer can help give some understanding of permanence. And I think there are some positive signs. Some people are beginning to see that they cannot go on looking for happiness in material accomplishments. This is a positive trend. I would hope that the Benedictine values become more widely known to the general public.

Sister

FIRMIN ESCHER

Born 1915

Sister Firmin is a member of the Benedictine community at St. Benedict's Monastery in St. Joseph, Minnesota.

❁

How deceptive appearances can be! An assistant leads Sister Firmin into the room, as her advanced glaucoma has left her with little sight. She seems frail and fragile, with porcelain skin and delicate, long fingers. Behind this fragile, gentle surface, however, is a woman of great strength and accomplishment. After more than twenty years of teaching, she was made the academic dean of the College of St. Benedict, and eleven years later she became the college's director of planning and program development. In that capacity she oversaw the difficult and ultimately successful cooperative merger of the College of St. Benedict and St. John's University. Then Sister Firmin was assigned the position of dean of fine arts and later became the director of planning for the monastery.

In addition to her deep love for teaching and music, she has always been willing to devote herself and to adapt. She never stopped learning and gaining more knowledge to better serve the college and her monastery and is a remarkable example of selfless dedication to the people she loves.

Sister Firmin

I COME FROM a family that prayed together. I went to an elementary school where Benedictine sisters taught, and I took music lessons from a wonderful sister who influenced me a great deal. I went to public high school for a year, but my mother and father didn't care for that very much. I was given a choice of Catholic high schools and I chose St. Benedict's Academy, which was here in St. Joseph. I gained firsthand knowledge of the life of the sisters — how they prayed and lived together. At the academy I studied piano with Sister Anastasia. She was a Native American woman and a very strict teacher. She influenced me greatly, and I respected her highly.

During my sophomore year at the academy, my sibling sister, Sister Wilma, made her final vows with the sisters at St. Benedict's. I sometimes think my sister prayed me into the order. By the end of the summer, I had made up my mind to be an aspirant. The aspirantship was for young women who were in high school and thinking about joining the religious life. We had classes in religion and did a great deal of housekeeping. During my second year in college at St. Benedict's I became a postulant, and in six months I received the habit and became a novice for one year. On July 11, 1935, I made triennial vows. I was then sent out to teach music, all instruments, in Eau Claire, Wisconsin. In 1938, I returned to the monastery and made my final vows.

I started teaching high school before I had a degree and before I made final vows. I really was still a kid myself when I taught in Eau Claire. I had a superior there who was very good but had one strange idea. Because I had some music training, she thought I could do everything there was to do in the area of teaching music. I simply had to teach myself as I went. Piccolo, timpani — you name it, I learned it and even wrote music for it.

After three years, I was called home to study violin seriously. The string teacher at the College of St. Benedict volunteered for mission work in China, and the prioress called in a violin teacher from Minneapolis to appraise the five sisters who played the violin and to decide who should go on to get a degree. To my surprise he picked me. To prepare for that degree, I stayed at St. Benedict's for a year to study liberal arts and also to do about a dozen other jobs. I taught the aspirants, the postulants, the novices, the day students, and so on. I also traveled to Minneapolis twice a week to take violin lessons. The next year I went to Minneapolis and studied full-time. In 1940, I was ready for the degree and that summer I gave my violin recital. I then started teaching at our college and continued to do so for twenty-one years. During that time, I spent four summers in Chicago and received my master's degree. I was also made chair of the department. I taught about everything that was teachable — orchestra, choral, opera. During the last eight years, we did a joint opera with St. John's University. I enjoyed teaching tremendously.

In 1961, after twenty-one years of teaching, I was made academic dean of the college. When I went in to the prioress for reassignment and she told me I was to be the dean, I told her I knew nothing of the area. She said I would learn, and I did. I was dean for eleven years and saw five presidents come and go. They were good years. I did so much learning. I went to many conferences and met many educators who became good friends and helped me a great deal. It was during this time that we began thinking about formal cooperation with

St. John's University so our students could take courses at either campus. I became very involved with that — chairing many committees and bringing in consultants.

In 1972 — I was now the director of planning and program development for the College of St. Benedict — I toured the country studying how other colleges were cooperating. I wrote cost analyses. I wrote planning grants and annual reviews. It was quite an experience. After five years I had a stroke. Fortunately, I had a speedy recovery and did a lot of physical therapy. The stroke affected my left arm and leg, and I worked with the violin a great deal to get my dexterity back. I had the stroke in June, and by December I played second violin in the orchestra for Handel's *Messiah.*

After my recovery, I was assigned to the position of dean of fine arts at the college. I was there for three years, and then the prioress asked me to begin a planning process for the monastery. So I left the college after forty years. It was a very different planning process than I had used at the college. It was much more participatory. Over the ten years I worked on planning, we had about 175 sisters engaged. Then in 1990 advanced glaucoma forced me to retire.

Looking back, I call myself a tumbleweed. I tumbled from one job to another. . . .

I have had many joys in my life, and if I were to pick major ones I would have one for *ora,* prayer, and one for *labora,* work. First, for *ora,* it would be the day of my final profession. I was so happy that I actually felt like I didn't want any company. It was rather selfish. The ceremonies in our day were so strong. There were thirty-three of us all making profession together.

As part of the ceremony, we were all fully prostrated on the sanctuary floor and we were all covered with a pall, a large piece of black cloth. Then four large funeral candles were put at the corners of the cloth. There we were trying to give our all. It was profound. The sisters prayed over us for a long time. I remember it was a hot day and the floor was cold. My breath made a little puddle on the floor where my nose was. When we all got up, there were thirty-three little puddles on the floor. On the *labora* side, my great joy was conducting. Orchestra, choral, all kinds of small groups — I loved them all. There is nothing like getting a whole group of people to make a beautiful sound.

I have, of course, also had some sorrows in my life, and again — were I to choose two — I would have one for *ora* and one for *labora.* For *ora,* I feel that during my years as a teacher and administrator I was not using my spiritual opportunities to the best of my abilities. I thought I was at the time, but because of my responsibilities, I was frequently absent from common exercises. Even when I was in choir, I was often distracted. I now feel very sad that I wasn't able to find a balance between prayer and work then. The most sorrowful aspect to my *labora* side was when I had to give up teaching in 1961. Plain and simple, I just didn't think it could happen.

In the Benedictine tradition, the Holy Rule is the foundation for everything that we do. We are guided by the vows of conversion of life, obedience, and stability.

At the center of our spiritual life are daily celebration of the Liturgy of the Hours and the Eucharist. *Lectio* and meditation are important daily exercises we gradually learn to love.

The prioress's monthly conferences have been very supportive in building on the spiritual foundation. Monthly days of retreat and classes in Benedictine spirituality are helpful in maintaining growth in our spiritual lives.

Another great aid to my spiritual life is the example of the sisters I live with. There is more prayer here than you can imagine. We have forty-three sisters who are over ninety years old. We are surrounded by prayer. I personally feel much more prayerful now than I did when I was younger. When you are young, it's easy to get wound up in your work. I'm very grateful for the time I now have to devote to my spiritual life. I must add that losing my sight twelve years ago has been a blessing. I now find inner sight in prayer. With the loss of my sight, I also lost many distractions.

St. Benedict's Rule has chapters to cover most physical aspects of life—eating, sleeping, clothing, and so on. We are to eat simple, balanced food at regular times. Clothing is also to be simple and fit properly. I wore the habit for thirty years. But when we had the opportunity to change from the stylized habit to lay clothing after Vatican II, I decided to change. You didn't have to; you had the choice. I found that the habit was a barrier to me in reaching other people. There was always a distance caused by the habit. I moved in higher education circles, and I noticed the difference immediately when I quit wearing the habit. It was a much easier exchange I could now have with people. We still dress simply; most of us wear second-hand clothes. As for sleeping, in Benedict's day they slept clothed in dormitories with elders in their midst. Well, we don't sleep in our day clothes, but I did spend many years in dormitories. With my educational duties I would often have to work beyond the nine o'clock lights-out time. I would tiptoe in the dark with a series of memorized steps in each direction to take me to my bed and very quietly got ready for bed. I did that for many years. Eventually we switched to three people per room, then two per room, and finally single rooms. I now live in an assisted-living group with fourteen other people. We all have our own rooms and share community and kitchen rooms. We have nurses to help when needed, but we still do a great deal on our own.

There are three chapters in the Rule that I would pick out as favorites. First, Chapter 2 on the qualities of the abbot and prioress. I am awed at the responsibilities we put on our leader. We give our prioress such great responsibilities that it gives us the obligation to try to do what we can to be of assistance to her. Both she and we must lead by example rather than word, and she and we must adjust ourselves to others' personalities. We must understand, excuse, and encourage one another. We can help the prioress by tending toward the qualities she possesses.

I also like Chapter 4 on the instruments of good works. It includes the Ten Commandments, the Golden Rule, the Beatitudes, some of the corporal and spiritual works of mercy, and some common sense. I find it so helpful. I like to have it read to me about twice a month. I find it jolts me in just the right place.

The other chapter is Chapter 7 on humility. It is a humdinger of a chapter. Some of the degrees of humility that Benedict describes I find impossible to deal with. It's a bit hard to swallow considering yourself as low as a worm or a beast in the field. To help with this I went to a couple of contemporary writers on the Rule, Sister Joan Chittister and the laywoman, Esther de Waal. Esther de Waal deals with humility in relation to obedience. Humility is really doing the will of God. To come to know God, you must lose your self-will and self-deceit. We deceive ourselves so easily. I have a lot of work to do on this myself.

Everything that stems from the Rule is a value. There is so much value in our community living—the sharing of the common table, the common prayers, supporting each other in our joys and sorrows.

Hospitality is of great value to Benedictines. Simplicity and humor are all values of our life. Certainly the art and music of the monastery are of great value. Art and music make us whole—they are civilizing forces.

I feel we must be aware of what is happening in the outside world. In the 1980s when we were working on community planning, I organized a multimedia event for the sisters dealing with the need for world vision and an understanding of global issues. I had eight slide projectors set up to project images of different subjects. I also had three movie projectors set up. We started them all up at once and let them run for about ten minutes. The sisters were in the middle and didn't know where to look or what to do. When we stopped the projectors you could have heard a pin drop. I tried to make the point that that's the way things are when we don't do planning and cannot focus. For the rest of the day, we went to panels and discussions on a wide variety of issues.

On a personal level, I have a daily prayer that I do for the world. It is a forty-minute litany of prayer. That ranges from my family, the sisters, the college, out to the entire world, being as specific as I can. I listen to the radio and pray for those in need. I ask God to put his arms around the world.

I have strong hopes for our community. Benedictines have had many ups and downs over the centuries. When they were down, there was usually a strong person who helped bring them back up. Our own community went through some serious struggles after Vatican II. We lost over one hundred sisters. But that loss pulled us together even more strongly than we were before. We are really still in somewhat of a transition, but I feel we are now toward the end of it. But we will never be a community of a thousand sisters again.

I believe that, in the future, laypeople are going to make an increasing contribution to religious life. This may take many forms, some which exist today such as associates and oblates, and in new ways that we aren't aware of yet. I see the possibility of women making shorter-term commitments. Laypeople are hungry for the spiritual life and will be doing more.

Brother

VICTOR J. FRANKENHAUSER

Born 1920

Brother Victor is a member of the Benedictine community at Assumption Abbey in Richardton, North Dakota.

Brother Victor's life and experience document a part of twentieth-century American Benedictine history that is all but lost now. Brother Victor was and still considers himself a lay brother. Until Vatican II in the 1960s, many male Benedictine communities had a two-tier system. One tier was made up of the ordained priest-monks, often considered the intellectual faction of the monastery. The second tier was formed by the lay brothers, who were not ordained and executed the lion's share of the manual labor in the monastery. In many monasteries the two groups were rather strictly segregated and had separate dining tables, separate sleeping quarters, separate recreation rooms, even separate areas for prayer. With the reforms of Vatican II, much of this two-tier system became eliminated. From a liberal point of view this would seem a positive development, bringing more equality to the monastery, but in Brother Victor's view these reforms and changes have been an attack on the unique identity and role of lay brothers. He feels that much has been lost in the transition.

Brother Victor

MY MOTHER CAME from south Russia. Her first husband died after they came to America, and she then married my father, who was from Germany. We were a large family and quite poor. I was born and grew up right here in Richardton, in the shadow of the abbey church steeples. I was a very small, self-conscious, and shy boy. I remember my first communion at the age of seven. I was so excited, as my parents had bought me a suit, and it had not only knickerbockers [short britches gathered at the knee], but also a pair of long trousers. I detested knickerbockers and was eagerly looking forward to wearing the long pants at my first communion. But my father said, "Since you insist on wearing the long trousers, you must wear the knickerbockers instead." I burst into tears and asked my mother to intercede for me, which she did, but in vain. I learned early in my life that my father's decision was always absolute and final. Father could never figure out why I was different from the other children.

I went to St. Mary's grade school that was staffed by the Benedictine sisters from Yankton, South Dakota. I drew great inspiration from the sisters. I didn't know much about the monks at the abbey, but the sisters were dedicated to their students. At the age of seven, I became an altar boy and approached the job with great dedication, sometimes serving at three or four masses in the morning and possibly a wedding or funeral later in the day. I would enjoy working with the slower priests so I could have more time to absorb all the rituals of the Mass. At home I would often "play priest" and sometimes hold my masses in the backyard.

In the sixth grade, we came across monks in our studies, and I looked them up in the *Catholic Encyclopedia.* I decided then and there that was what I wanted to be in my life. In the eighth grade I suffered from melancholia and did not feel I was doing well in school. My relationship with my father did not improve. I feared him more than ever. I won a writing contest for an essay on "Why I should become a Priest." And I received a book as a gift from the abbot. This cheered me for a while, but my low moods persisted. My mother, as always, was my solace. She would encourage me, but also chide me at times for being so sensitive and for taking life so seriously.

After eighth grade the boys were sent to the abbey for high school. Of the boys I graduated with from eighth grade, about half of them went on to high school, and half of them went back to the farm. It was the Depression years and many could not afford school. Our family was also unable to pay my way, so I applied to the abbey to work in the kitchen to support myself. At first they were reluctant to take me on as I weighed only sixty-five pounds. But they did give me the job, and I got up with the monks every morning at 4:40 a.m. I went to Morning Prayer with the brothers, and at 6:00 a.m. I went to the kitchen to help prepare breakfast and wash dishes until classes started at 8:00 a.m. Then at noon I helped with kitchen duties, and again at 4:00 p.m. I was back in the kitchen until after supper, when I had study hall, then to bed. I also worked for them during the summer for room and board and tuition. I drew great inspiration from the brothers whom I worked with. They were mostly Swiss and Germans and wonderful friends and role models. Because the brothers were not ordained, they were called lay brothers.

I felt a great deal of stress trying to get my studies done well, and in my senior year of high school I decided that the rigors of preparing for the priesthood were not for me. But I still very much wanted to serve the Lord in some useful way, so I leaned toward joining the brothers. I had really grown up with them. My father was at first vehemently against my desire to become a brother. He worked at the abbey power plant and saw the brothers as "lower-class citizens" from the priests. But in time he came around and offered little resistance to my joining. In 1939, I took my vows to join the brothers as a monk of Assumption Abbey. We made three-year temporary vows after a one-year novitiate. Then in 1943 I made my perpetual vows. I did not see him, but the abbot told me my father was in the last row of the church during the ceremony, so he had somewhat reconciled himself to my decision. When I joined the brothers I was one of only four American-born brothers; all the rest were from Europe. At that time, the priests and the lay brothers had separate sleeping quarters in the monastery, separate areas for prayer, separate tables in the refectory, separate recreation rooms, and the brothers had no vote in the chapter meetings. Brothers and priests were prohibited from socializing together on a regular basis.

In the monastery one does what needs to be done. I had about ten music lessons in my life, but I ended up serving as monastery organist and also gave piano lessons to students. In those days the abbot said, "You can do it." And you did.

From my very first days in the monastery, I worked in the print shop doing bookbinding and typesetting. I was then also assigned to the sacristy. It was a big job — laying out vestments for twenty-five priests, setting up for the Eucharist, preparing the altar, and cleaning the church. There were many duties. It was a daily task that demanded unfailing exactitude, reverence, and respect for details. Everything had its proper place, and responsibility and punctuality were imperative. I was twenty-one years in that position, and it was one of the most rewarding experiences of my life in the monastic community. Then came the 1960s and Vatican II. I wasn't comfortable with all the changes that took place in the liturgy. All the order that we had followed was changed to disorder.

The abbot then asked me to be guestmaster instead of the sacristy work. The abbot thought it would be good for my shyness if I started to work more with people. I wasn't so sure, but he said to try it. I now feel it is my calling. It was a second calling that was to become more demanding than my first calling. I have always had low self-esteem, probably due to the relationship I had with my father, but the monastery got me counseling assistance that helped me in my new position and in other ways, too. So, for the last thirty years, I have been working with the guests, giving tours of the monastery, and often working the monastery telephone switchboard. Because I started serving Mass here at the age of seven, I have one of the longest histories with the abbey, and have known all the monks of the abbey except the first fourteen who passed away before I started.

My roots are in a Benedictine parish. The teachers of my elementary and high school years were Benedictines, and they instilled a sense of Benedictine spirituality in us. The pastors at the church here have always been Benedictines. This preparation led me first to want to save my soul, second to be helpful to others, and third to search for God. I was inspired to want to live the Christian life to the fullest. Here at the monastery the center is God in both *ora* and *labora.* Liturgical prayer combines all forms of prayer. The Divine Office is a primary part of that, but the brothers didn't say the Office until 1942; we had a different prayer structure from the Divine Office of the priests. Then St. John's Abbey in Collegeville, Minnesota, compiled and printed *The Short Breviary* in the early 1940s. When I heard it was available, I went to the abbot and asked if we brothers could use it. He said he wondered if we would ever come and ask, as he had already ordered the books.

In my private prayer I have a longing for silence, and I do most of my prayer in my room. We have lost much of the silence we used to have in the community. All meals used to be in silence, few are now.

I've always felt that silence is one of the great lessons of the Rule. Loudness, harshness, and rowdiness have no place in the monastery. There seems to be more acceptance of that today, but I feel there needs to be reverence and decorum in our life.

St. Benedict was moderate in the way he structured his Rule. I feel I could not be a Trappist, with their meatless diets and fasting. I don't think I could do that. Benedict structured a system in which you could lead a fuller Christian life. I am still learning from the Rule. I am still striving to perfect myself with the Rule. There are always new dimensions of the Rule to learn. I'm proud to be a Benedictine.

I had learned punctuality and manners already from the sisters in school, and that was an important part of our physical life at the monastery. Etiquette and manners have always been important to me.

When I came to the monastery during the Depression, the food was very frugal. Today we have more variety. The

German and Swiss monks were meat-and-potato people. We certainly have always gotten enough to eat, and people did not go away hungry. St. Benedict states in his Rule that all eating and drinking is to be done in moderation. In the old days we ate separated: the priests at tables according to their rank in the community, the seminarians and novices, and then the lay brothers. This seems strange in today's society, but it was a system that worked well for me. I believe God created me specifically to be a lay brother. It is my calling in life. When Vatican II came and eliminated so many of the distinctions between lay brothers and priests in the community, I felt we brothers lost much of our identity. I'm afraid that when lay brothers who developed in the monasteries during the 1940s and 1950s pass away, there will be no one left who remembers what it was like to truly be a lay brother in the old way. In many ways I feel the lay brothers were the real monks of the monastery, as they were home at the monastery doing the everyday work. They kept the home fires burning. The priests were many times busy teaching, going to school, or doing parish work. Our abbot for many years, Abbot Cuthbert, used to come back from visitations to other monasteries and call our brothers the "cream of the crop." About the only requirement for a brother at that time was that the candidate truly seek God and could contribute some useful service to the monastery. Among them were the most dedicated and sincere monks one could find anywhere. I'm concerned all they did will be forgotten. When the changes first took place, I isolated myself and refused to cooperate, but by doing so I only brought more sorrow on myself. I felt I needed to stand up for the traditions that were a deep part of my life. It may seem strange to protest against the changes that seemed to give brothers more rights and equality with the priests, but

I saw the old traditions forming a distinct type of vocation for the brothers that was taken away by the changes. It was a vocation I dearly loved. It took me many years to adapt to the changes. I could not leave. Even in the hardest times for me, this is where I've always wanted to be. I was called to this place and this life.

I lived only thirteen years at home. All the other years I have been in this monastery. At times I felt like I had missed some of my boyhood days, but I wouldn't exchange the experience I had for anything. I have been fortunate to be here. I don't think I could have handled many of the huge changes of the twentieth century that have taken place in the outside world. I am baffled by computers. I have never driven a car. I tried once and it was a disaster. I have a fear that I might hurt someone while driving. How could I live with that? I have been blessed to be here. I feel I am where God wants me to be. When I get depressed I sometimes think about the shortness of life compared with eternity, and I count my blessings. What gives me joy today is being of service to others. I enjoy giving tours and telling people some of our history. I also greatly enjoyed my work in the sacristy. Being of service is a joy.

There are values which are important for our well-being. The Ten Commandments are ten values that help us live a better life, and they need to be promoted so we can live as good a life as human conditions permit.

I also put a great value on confession. It perks me up spiritually. It is so easy to fall into the same faults. I always thought that when I reached sixty it would be easier, but it wasn't. I throw tantrums sometimes. You might not believe it, but I do.

I also find value in simplicity—in living the simple life. It was one of the things I liked about the life of the lay brother. It was a life of sincerity and straightforward relations. If anyone had a bone to pick with you, they did it then and there and it was over with — no grudges held.

I do have hopes for the future. Certainly the monastic life will go on. The new system has created a new kind of monk different from the lay brother of my time. It has created a gap in the community, and there is now more need for lay help and associates. I hope some of the traditions will return. The future is in the hands of God.

Sister

LILLIAN HARRINGTON

Born 1918

Sister Lillian is a member of the Benedictine community at Mount St. Scholastica Monastery in Atchison, Kansas.

As I meet Sister Lillian in her office, I become immediately aware that she is not your "traditional" Benedictine sister. Sister Lillian is nicely dressed in a dark blue suit, not unusual since Vatican II, but she is also wearing jewelry and what appear to be traces of makeup. It turns out Sister Lillian has many wonderful and rather unusual qualities. Filling the role of "rabbi" to a group of "priest-less" Catholics is just one of the progressive hats Sister Lillian wears. Her long experience with public speaking gives her a dynamic presence. She talks with confidence, clarity, and conviction. She has a sense of authority that makes one quickly aware that she is a force to be reckoned with.

Sister Lillian

I GREW UP near the small town of Blaine, Kansas, about sixty miles from here. Sisters from Mount St. Scholastica taught at our high school, and my mother used to bring them eggs and other items to help them get by. I would often accompany my mother on her trips when I was about three or four years old. I recall two of the sisters clearly, Sister Anthony, one of the teachers, and a Sister Irmingard who was the housekeeper. I remember saying to my mother that I wanted to be a sister, but I didn't want to be a Sister Irmingard; I wanted to be a Sister Anthony. I can still hear myself saying that. I don't remember what I had against poor Sister Irmingard, but I wasn't going to be that sister. I didn't know anything about sisters, but I used to play at being one. I would get my mother's dishtowels and put them on my head and walk around the house. I would teach school, and my dolls were my students. I started making report cards out then. Little did I know I would still be making them out sixty-five years later.

I attended a one-room country school and I went through grade school rapidly, often taking several grades at a time. Back then, I thought it was a really great thing, but later I found out it wasn't so great. I started the high school where the sisters were teaching at the age of twelve. I tried to be like the older students, and I think it made me very dependent on other people's opinions of me. I graduated at the age of sixteen. I liked sisters as teachers but I really didn't know anything about them. We had a retreat before graduation and one of the priests made a comment that maybe I should become a sister. I left that summer to join Mount St. Scholastica. I was sixteen years old. I knew nothing about what I was getting into. I had never heard the word "monastic." I just picked up and left like Abraham. But Abraham had a special call, and I certainly didn't know I did. Some sisters talk about their special call to come. I didn't recognize it as a call. I was simply young and naive. I was a child, a real child. When I was in my early forties, I began to question why I was let into the monastery at such a young age. I had a real angry spell because I thought I missed some growing up. It's impossible to say what would have become of me had I not come here, but I don't think I would have had the opportunities and interaction with people that being Benedictine has given me.

I was a blank page when I came. They could do anything they liked with me. I think of what the women who come to our monastery go through today when they enter. They stay for a while and people visit with them and they are taught about religious life. I knew nothing. I was one of six young girls. I don't think my parents would have let me marry at that age, but they let me come here. Now we have nine years before you have to make up your mind. In those days we had six months, and it was "ready or not here we come." After six months, we got the habit. We didn't say "entering the novitiate" in those days. I received the new name of Mary William, which I used from 1934 to 1967 when we were allowed to return to our baptismal names. First vows were made a year after getting the habit. So why did I become a Benedictine? I just came, fell in, and stayed.

I love teaching, and I know that I can be an excellent teacher. My greatest gift in teaching is being able to empower the people I teach — to help them bring out their gifts. It reminds me of the story of a woodcarver in ancient China. The carver made a bell stand that was so beautiful the people were awed, and they thought it must be the work of spirits. But the carver explained his carving as follows, "After three days of fasting I forgot about success or failure, after five days of fasting I forgot about praise or criticism, and after seven days of fasting I forgot about the emperor and his court. Then I went into the forest and went from tree to tree until I found the tree that already had the bell stand within it. All I had to do was put it in my hand and release it. What you call the work of spirits is the union of my contemplative spirit and the nature of the tree that released the bell stand." This story powerfully says what a teacher should be, to look for the bell stands in her or his students, release them, and let them be.

When I began, we were a teaching order. I knew that I was going to teach, and that was fine with me. I had started with my little dolls a long time ago. I didn't have a full semester of college training when I was sent to replace a teacher who had gotten sick. I was seventeen years old, and I taught third and fourth grade in a little town called Shawnee. I did not even have a full year of college after that. All my degrees were obtained in summer school. I continued in grade school teaching for quite a while and then taught high school until 1969. I then taught English, speech, and Bible literature at Penn Valley Community College in Kansas City, Missouri, for eighteen years. Teaching and retreat work were and are a joy.

I retired from teaching in 1988 at the age of seventy. It was forced retirement in those days. After that retirement I joined Sister Mary Austin working in the Archdiocese Office of the Aging, working with the elderly. I worked with her for three years, and then she died from cancer. I took over the office for a year, but I told them I would do it for only a year. In the meantime I became what I call a "pilgrim minister." Because of my speech background, I started training lectors (enabling the laity to proclaim the Scripture at the Eucharist) and also Eucharistic ministers and ministers of hospitality. I have since trained many people to be trainers as well. I more or less trained myself out of a job. For the past three years I have been on the Mount St. Scholastica Sophia Center staff where we organize workshops, retreats, mentoring, weeks of Benedictine experience, twelve-step programs, and spiritual direction. I have been blessed with good health and energy, and doing workshops tends to give me more energy. The director tells me that last year I went to seventy-seven sites doing retreats or workshops and probably reached about four to five thousand people.

One of the other things I do is to serve a priest-less Catholic group in Kansas City, Missouri. They celebrate the Seder meal on Holy Thursday, and for the past ten years I have been their "rabbi." They are a close, outgoing community oriented toward social justice. I enjoy that commitment very much.

One of these days I will probably have to slow down, but until then — so long as I have the energy — I will keep "pilgriming." I love to proclaim the Word.

The Rule tells us that our lives are a pilgrimage; we are seeking God. We are on a search, and I'm still searching. The Rule provides the means for the search. In high school the sisters taught us to put these wonderful letters at the top of our papers, *UIOGD* (*Ut In Omnibus Glorificetur Deus*), Latin initials for "That in all things God may be glorified," which is from the gospel and the Rule. Two other great Benedictine mottos are *ora et labora,* pray and work, and the simplest Benedictine motto, *pax,* peace; these mottos are channels, paths for the search that Benedict set up. He also structured the vows that we take. When I made vows, we professed poverty, chastity, obedience, stability, and conversion of life. Today they don't name poverty and chastity.

Benedict starts the Rule with the word "Listen," which is what obedience is all about. We need to listen as God speaks through Scripture, through nature, the events of our lives, the prioress, and through one another. Benedict is very precise that we must be obedient to one another. Benedict gives us the means for the search along with a life of balance. He structures a balance of prayer, work, holy reading, and leisure. But the key for the search for me has been an absolute openness to life — whatever happens. This is a personal approach that relates to what happened in my first years of religious life. In the first seventeen years of my religious life, I was assigned to nineteen different places. I shouldn't have, perhaps, but I even asked my superior why I was moved every year. She said that with some people she had to move them every year, and some people would simply fit in anywhere, and I was among the latter. It was kind of sweet, but I was dumb enough to tell some of the other sisters and they razzed me about it. But that mobile experience had an impact on me. I lived with nineteen different groups of women. I learned to adapt and give in when needed. It has actually made me desire change, and it was an enriching experience.

The Divine Office always supplied the rhythm of the day, even when it was in Latin. But we kept adding things on: all kinds of acts of prayers and all kinds of litanies, until in prayer the externals became important for me. Then wonderful Vatican II came. It was an exciting time and a time of great flux. We started changing our dress and having more English in the Mass and Office. We had all kinds of experimentation. It was almost as if we didn't know who we were. Vatican II called us to go back to our own charism, and that is when we went back and really rediscovered the Rule. This was when we formulated our "Call to Life." It was a reformulating of our constitution. It became much less formal and rigid. Instead of being a group of women being shaped by rigid rules, we became a group of individuals being shaped by the gospel and the Rule. The basis to our life is our community, seeking God through prayer and ministry. I didn't realize how important common prayer was to me until I found myself studying with a group of women religious who didn't have this tradition, and I realized how much it had become a part of me and how much I missed it. Community living and communal prayer are very basic to our spiritual development.

When I was fifty-nine, I received a call to conversion — a spiritual change in my life. It may be that it was really my call to religious life and all that had gone on before was preparing me. After Vatican II, we changed to personal *lectio,* spiritual reading, and reflection. This was a challenge and very important for my spiritual growth. Vatican II was a joyous time with all that experimental living.

My spiritual life is very much caught up in community. Community is like breathing out and breathing in. I could not live alone. I find God in people. In the Scriptures it says that if you can't find God in the people you can see, how can you love God whom you cannot see? God is among us. I find the hospitality of Benedict in receiving everyone as Christ very logical because that is who they are. We try to see Christ in everything. One of the things I do since I came home, back to the monastery, three years ago is to help in the laundry. I work there every morning for about an hour. I fold the nightgowns. As I was working one morning I thought of Benedict's teaching that everything should be treated as the vessels of the altar, and I began thinking that each of those women who were in those gowns last night was Christ. It made the folding so meaningful. I could see those elderly women who may have needed to be changed two or three times a night, and their bodies are the body of Christ.

In our spiritual lives I believe we need to steep ourselves in beauty. To cut beauty and art out of our lives is to diminish ourselves. Beauty does something to our lives just as ugliness does something to our lives. Ours is a community of very highly educated and gifted women. I can always find someone with the gift I might be in need of, and people are always willing to share their gifts.

My spirituality would be seeing all of life: the contemplative, the silence (which I used to hate), the manual labor, the Divine Office, the community, the hospitality, and art and learning are all one piece. All of that is a way of trying to find God. I can't find God in a vacuum. I have to find God in the events of my life. People are windows of good. They enrich my life. But my search for God has sometimes been a process of sorrow. Sometimes I yearn so strongly for God that it is painful. But I guess if I found God completely, the search would be over, and the whole thing is about the search for God. I don't think we can ever wholly find God, or we would be God.

The Rule of Benedict is the guiding light on my pilgrimage. The Prologue, which is so beautiful, calls us to seek God. The reception of guests is very important to me. I believe much of our lives can be formed by the models we see as children. My mother was the pinnacle of hospitality. No one could enter the house without sitting down to have a cup of coffee, whether they wanted to or not. It was a part of her nature. I assumed that was the way everyone treated people.

Another aspect of the Rule that is very important to me is Benedict's insistence on the care of the elderly and sick. I need to do better on this point. I need to spend more time with the elderly sisters. The Rule stresses the value of human life—who we are and not what we do. The Rule's emphasis on mutual obedience even in the little things is so important, even when one has to give up one's own desires to make the whole thing work. Coming from the first word of the Rule, listening is one of the greatest values. Many times it's listening for what's not said, or as Benedict said, listening with the "ear of the heart." To understand the pain of some people who cannot express the pain, I have to learn to listen to what they are *not* saying. It's also very important to listen to what people *are* saying. I know I've caught myself figuring out what I'm going to say when I should be listening to what's being said. That's not the kind of listening we need to do. *Lectio* is a discipline of listening to God. I know I need to listen to the events of my life, to nature, to the poor, and to be an open listener—to learn to listen to those with whom I don't agree and not selectively tune them out.

I think there is a great cry and hunger in the world for the value of community. We can be a model for that value. The Benedictine values of hospitality, stability, and silence are also values that the outside world can benefit from.

Reverence that encompasses the earth, food, utensils, furniture, and especially people is a key value. We need to affirm one another. We need genuine caring for one another. We need to accept people for who they are and not for what we would like them to be. Sometimes that's tough.

Manual labor is an important value to uphold. Three of our well-educated young women have opted to do maintenance work rather than seek professional work outside the monastery. In the past I think we have looked down somewhat on some manual labor, like housekeeping. We now, for the most part, are overcoming that. We have so many values in our community: balance, celebration, prayer, beauty, simplicity, education, authority, service, and commitment are all important in our lives.

Knowing that everyone is Christ has created my attitude toward the outside world. God has given me many gifts, but the greatest has been the ability to share my gifts with the outside world. Our ministry flows out of our communal life. Monasticism should be a wellspring for nurturing faith. We are so accustomed to our life here that we can't see it, but people who come and visit say they can't get over our hospitality. But some people can't come here, so there is the need to go out to the people as well. We have a secondhand store for the poor, we have a Head Start program, and a GED program, all to help the larger community.

Fifty-seven years of my sixty-four years here have been spent doing mission work, but there was always the connection back to the monastery. The Sophia Center is now one of the primary ministries of the monastery, and I'm happy to be a part of it.

The regularity of the monastery has certainly helped promote good health. Three good balanced meals a day and available health care promotes well-being. The flexibility of the lifestyle is also healthy. You learn to go with the flow. Change is not hard for me. I'm deadened without change. I think Vatican II did a great deal for our emotional health. It made us realize we are women and that we are individuals in a communal setting, not carbon copies of one another.

I have many hopes for the future. I have personal hopes, community hopes, church hopes, and world hopes. My personal hope is that when the time comes I can let go of my activities with grace and joy. I also hope I can increase my faith, to persevere in the search, to keep looking for the question and being at peace. I hope I can be there for whoever needs me.

My community hopes are that, although I know we will never have great numbers of members, I hope women will continue to come and embrace and carry on the charism. I also hope that our Sophia Center, which is really beginning to take hold, will be embraced as the community ministry and will carry the spirit of Benedict to a larger area. I hope the monastery will be open to creative new ways to grow and carry on our traditions and missions.

My hope for the church is to see a reinstatement of the principles of Vatican II. We are losing them, and the church seems to be going backwards. I think the day has to come when women and married men can become priests. I think the priesthood itself needs to change. I think it needs to expand to where the communities themselves select their own priests. I perceive the hierarchy to be power-hungry and oppressive. They need to get back to what Jesus was about two thousand years ago. We need to understand that the laity is the church. They are what the church is for.

My hope for the world is peace — that somehow we can learn to solve difficulties with diplomatic means. While we will always have some poverty, the rich nations need to realize that what we have is only ours as stewards and we need to share our good fortune. We need to have a form of forgiveness similar to that of the ancient Jewish jubilee, where all is forgiven and a fresh start is begun.

Sister

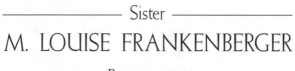

M. LOUISE FRANKENBERGER

Born 1916

Sister Louise is a member of the Olivetan Benedictine community at Holy Angels Convent in Jonesboro, Arkansas.

Holy Angels' contemporary design blends into the convent's 160 acres of rolling wooden hills. When Sammy and I meet Sister Louise, she wears her off-white garment that is characteristic of the Olivetan Benedictine Sisters of Holy Angels. She is the most gentle of people. Her quiet demeanor and modesty reflect the sense of harmony she has found living in this most supportive community. During our breaks, Sammy and I explore the grounds. The azaleas are in full bloom, with cascades of red, pink, and white. Squirrels scamper and play around us as we stroll through the serene woods. It is hard for us to believe that only a month before our visit, two children at a Jonesboro middle school opened fire on their classmates, killing four students and one teacher, and wounding eleven. This harsh contrast of the peace inside the convent and the violence outside is a continuous part of the fifteen-hundred-year-old history of the Benedictines.

Sister Louise

My father worked in the oil fields of Oklahoma. That is where I was born. In 1922, we moved to New Mexico due to my father's health problems. I started my education there at a school run by Franciscan sisters. We then returned to Oklahoma, and soon after my father died, after which we moved back to my mother's hometown, Pocahontas in Arkansas. Momma took in laundry and couldn't have made more than fifteen dollars a week. I don't see how she ever took care of us. My sister and I began attending St. Paul's School, which was run by the sisters from Holy Angels Convent. I remember the Franciscan sisters in New Mexico wore brown habits that weren't very appealing to me, but the Benedictines here wore white and I liked that. The sisters were very nice to us after Daddy died. I became especially close to one who became my third-grade teacher. She was so graceful in her white flannel habit. I thought I'd really like to be someone like that. I remember at my confirmation the bishop asked how many girls would like to be nuns, and I raised my hand just enough for him to see. After we got home my mother said it was strange that the bishop had said that six girls had raised their hands and she could only see five. I didn't tell her the sixth hand was mine. The sisters then invited me to go to their academy here in Jonesboro to finish my high school education. In my junior year at the academy, I asked the mother superior six times if I could join the community. Every time she would say that I should wait another month. I was very appreciative to the sisters for paying for my junior and senior year of high school. In 1933, I entered the convent at the age of seventeen. I had a wonderful novitiate director.

I made my first vows in 1935 and was sent to our hospital to work. It was a shock to me as I really didn't think of myself as becoming a nurse. I entered the nursing school we had there and started studying to be a lab technician. Well, I liked it but things didn't work out just right. In three months, I was switched to teaching fifth and sixth grade. I walked into the school and a sister showed me two stacks of books, one for fifth grade and one for sixth grade. She said that they would be my books for the rest of the year. I told her I wasn't a teacher, and she said I was going to be. Well, I made it through the year and then started my summer school training to be a teacher. Come to think of it, I started going to summer school in 1936 and was still in summer school in 1986. I thought I'd never get out. In my career I taught at many different schools and taught many different grades and subjects. I was also novitiate director for twelve years. I was so surprised when I was first assigned to the job that I took the letter to the superior and asked if it had been addressed incorrectly, but it wasn't a mistake.

I was made chemistry and biology teacher at the high school in Pocahontas. I went to night school to learn the information I needed. I studied psychology and also got a degree in counseling. I finally finished with a master's degree in biology. For fifteen years in Pocahontas, I was also what we call the moderator of the house. I took care of all the day-to-day chores of the house, paying the bills, seeing to the upkeep, and making sure everyone got the medical care they needed.

When I was in my fifties, I felt a very special closeness to God. It was a freedom of the spirit. It was as if one were on an escalator, being moved higher and higher. It was a time of great peace of heart.

When I was around sixty, I had about five different classes to prepare for daily at the school I was teaching at, and I was also in charge of the school library. It was just too much. I tried to explain to the priest in charge of the school that I was overloaded, but he just said I would get by. It was crushing. Another sorrow was that after all the work I had done with the novices, the years of the late sixties came and many left. It was very hard to go through, but it was happening all over.

When I was eighty years old, the mother superior came over to Pocahontas and asked if I wanted to retire. Well, I was feeling a bit achy, so I thought it over and said that I was ready to come home to the motherhouse. I now make dresses for poor girls that we give out at Easter. Since 1985, I have also made twenty-five quilts. People give me the patterns they want and I make them. I also supervise our gift shop, where we sell needlework and other items the sisters make.

My home life laid the foundation for my Benedictine life. We had no desire to party or socialize. We wanted to stay at home. Mother did a great deal of sewing, and she taught us to sew as well and we helped her with her work. We also prayed together daily. We were poor, but we really didn't know it. Before we went to school in the morning, we helped Mother get ready for the day's washing. Sunday afternoon was a little retreat. She would spread a blanket out under a shade tree, and we would do spiritual reading. We had poverty and obedience as part of our family life. We also had stability in the family as well; we stayed put. It was a good basis for Benedictine life.

As children we fished for food and raised a big garden, and we ate good, sensible food. It is the same here, a real sensible physical life. We live a life with a rhythm that combines the physical and the spiritual. An ordinary day of mine looks like this: I get up at 5 a.m.; meditation is at 5:30; morning group prayer at 6:00; breakfast at 6:30; piano practice (I'm learning to play the piano) at 7:00; then after 8 a.m. I do laundry and quilting; 11:30 a.m. — personal prayer; 11:45 a.m. — noon group prayer; at 12 noon, we have lunch; the afternoon is free to work on quilting or other sewing; 4:30 p.m. — adoration/spiritual reading; 5:00 p.m. is Mass; at 6:00 p.m., we have supper; 6:30 p.m. — recreation, quilting/sewing; 8:00 p.m. — group evening prayer; and bedtime is between 9:00 and 10:00 p.m.

I don't spend much time watching television. I watch it once in a while, and when you hear of the great poverty, violence, and sorrow in the world it cuts me to the heart. All I can do is pray. I have a tender regard for those in trouble, and my heart especially goes out to little children. If I had another life to live and plenty of money, I would like to take in every baby without a home and give them all the love and care I could.

It's probably not right, but I thank God I'm not in the outside world. I'm so thankful to be in the religious life.

I think we need more respect for superiors — to watch the way you talk. Some young people don't understand the proper respect that needs to be shown. I remember in our first constitution it was written that when young women joined our convent they were to be trained as elite ladies. They were to be trained in the arts. We also need to respect one another and be very helpful toward others. We need to look out for the needs of others. That's when we are living together like real Benedictine sisters.

That relates nicely to Chapter 72 of the Rule of Benedict on "the good zeal." It's based on the idea of helping others when you are able to do so. It's about little things like holding the door open when someone is coming behind you. Another example: I enjoy sewing for the sisters.

The chapter on silence is also a favorite of mine. I love the silence of our lives. It creates a time when your attention can be called to spiritual matters and what is truly good.

When I think of the future, I am aware our numbers are going down. I think at Holy Angels we're down to fifty-three sisters now. Some of the sisters fear that the community will dwindle to nothing. I argue that we must trust in God. We are doing God's work. Yes, we need to prepare for times with fewer sisters, but I feel great things can still happen, and we don't need enormous numbers to do good work. We need to go back to our basics even though we are doing new things. I don't think it is so much what we believe that will happen, but what God has in mind for us that will happen. We will have some hardships, and we will need the wisdom to guide us under God's direction.

Father

BERNARD SANDER

Born 1918

Father Bernard is a member of the Benedictine community at Mount Angel Abbey in St. Benedict, Oregon.

❁

As Sammy and I drive up the hill to Mount Angel Abbey, I come to understand that its name is well chosen. The view from the abbey is beautiful. The rolling green land is all around us, dissolving into the distant Oregon mist that gives us the feeling of being perched on a lush green island. Father Bernard's many years as guest master and director of oblates are apparent in every aspect of his demeanor. He is the personification of Benedictine openness and hospitality. He is full of kind words and concern for our welfare, but his warm welcome is equally reflected in the gentleness of his eyes and in his whole being. He truly radiates a heartfelt welcome.

Father Bernard

I GREW UP in Tillamook here in Oregon. Catholicism in our family goes back to Europe, with German roots on my father's side and Swiss roots on my mother's side. There were priests and nuns on both sides of the family. My grandfather came from Germany and ended up caring for his brother's seven children as well as his own seven children after his brother's death. He moved to Oregon because he saw the German-language paper published by Mount Angel Abbey. The priest in Tillamook had put in an ad asking for good German Catholic families to move to the community. My grandfather saw the ad, responded, and came. It was a difficult life, and they were exploited by uncaring people. But they themselves were strong and wonderful. My mother and father were living in Ashland, Oregon, and moved back to Tillamook because of the Catholic school for us children. If they hadn't done that, I doubt I would have become a priest. I owe them so much. My father would go to any ends to make sure we attended that school. There was some prejudice against Catholics in the community, and the school board refused to let us ride the school bus. We lived on a dairy farm some miles out of town. In his determination, my father managed to get my older brother, who was fourteen at the time, a driver's license to take us to school. To make matters more complicated, on the way to school we also took the milk to the cheese factory every morning and picked up the whey to feed the pigs on our way home.

More influences on my decision to become a monk and priest were that the parish in Tillamook was staffed by Benedictines. My father's brother was a priest and a great one. He was deeply loved and respected. When I came to the seminary here at Mount Angel, I was probably more interested in becoming a priest of the diocese than a monk. By my third year here I needed to make up my mind whether I would be a Benedictine or a diocesan priest. In my three years of study here, I had been very much taken with the life of the monastic community, particularly the prayer life. In those years we had a supremely beautiful Latin Gregorian chant routine. It had a resonance in my soul for some reason. I was taken by the life of prayer but worried about what I was going to do in a monastic cell all day long. I told my concerns to one of the older Benedictine priests and in his understanding way he said, "But my dear, you know, we do have a school and a retreat house here." As things turned out, I landed in both of them.

In the fall of 1938, I joined the novitiate here. I took my first vows in 1939, final vows in 1942, and was ordained in 1944.

In the fall of 1945, I was appointed as the assistant rector to the seminary at Mount Angel. In those days we didn't have a variety of high-power degrees. I learned everything I needed to know for the job by sliding on the seat of my pants. I also taught high school classes about fifteen hours a week. I was extremely busy. A great deal of keeping the discipline of the seminary was based on the monastic structure.

My job as assistant rector dealt with the spiritual and character formation of the students. In my early days of working with the seminarians, I was very frustrated by not having more background in dealing with the problems of young people. I probably expected more from some of those people than they were able to do. It has been a sorrow to me that I didn't know better. Fortunately, with studies I would shortly do at the University of Notre Dame, I became more effective.

We also started a school paper and a mothers' club to give the seminarians more contact with the students' families. In my second year as assistant rector, I came down with tuberculosis — overwork. I took a year off, recovered, and was back at work the next year. I then did several years of summer study at Notre Dame and learned about Catholic Action, which was a practical application of theology to everyday life. I really enjoyed it. It changed my whole outlook on ministry. I brought these ideas back to the West Coast and helped get them going here. The application took three forms: the Young Christian Students for high school and college people, the Young Christian Workers for unmarried wage earners, and the Christian Family Movement. These three organizations of Catholic Action began to be used all around the country with positive results. There was a lot of wonderful work that went on and beautiful people who helped and learned. It was a very practical approach to bringing life and religion together. I worked in Catholic Action until about 1966. I was blessed with the support of the abbot. Then when Vatican II came along, we thought all the problems would be solved and we mistakenly let up on these organizations, and they all kind of melted away.

In 1952, I had become rector of various aspects of the school, and that lasted until 1970. I then became the abbey guestmaster and retreat director for over twenty years. I began many programs in those years. I really enjoyed the work. We now have retreat programs for married couples, iconographers, lawyers and spouses, women, artists, mothers and daughters, marriage encounters, private retreats, and others.

In 1981, I moved to the position of director of oblates where I give spiritual direction for laypeople. The oblates are laypeople who wish to be extended members of our praying community. They have a very personal relationship with the monastery and attempt to follow the Rule of St. Benedict as best they can in their own lives. We have six retreats for oblates a year. They can pray with the monks whenever they want. We now have over 475 oblates. They have a real sense of pride in our community.

Supporting people so they can truly become people has given me joy. In giving spiritual direction, I can help people find their potential. Some people need to be shown that they have potential. Once people do find themselves, there is no stopping them. I have also received so much enjoyment from friendship, both in and outside of the community. People have also done a great deal to help me grow. I've been blessed with so much affirmation along the way. When I celebrated my fiftieth year since ordination, seven hundred people showed up. It was a wonderful day.

At the monastery the rhythm of the prayer life is the foundation for our spiritual life: at 5:30 a.m., we have early prayer; at 6:00 a.m., Holy Readings; Lauds at 6:30; Mass at 8:00; 12:00, Noon Prayer; 5:15 p.m., Vespers; and Compline at 7:30 p.m. There is a security in the stability of the schedule — a stability in the family of the Benedictines.

The Holy Prayer is so significant. The Rule of St. Benedict teaches me to see things through — to not back off when things get tough. The Rule teaches me a sense of meaningful obedience, an obedience that has a true sense of satisfaction in it. The Rule has a tremendous sense of balance in it. There is not a sense of the heroic. It is about being faithful to answer that bell — day after day, year after year, decade after decade.

The Rule and this life can teach you to go beyond yourself and your own soul to work for the true blessing of having God bless others.

The consistency in our prayer life and the responsibilities we have are very important. St. Benedict talks a lot about reverence. We need respect for the personhood of people, respect for who God is. The respect for people needs to be very long and very deep. For example, in the dining room we are placed according to the year we joined the community. If you are positioned next to a guy who slurps his soup, you could be listening to that for a long time. We have to make allowance for the weaknesses of others. Accepting people's differences and weaknesses is a way to become holy. Benedict is very clear on this. He will not put up with any murmuring or grumbling. This is how Benedict wants us to become holy: not through harsh fasting or the like but through the daily contact we have with each other. If you look at your married life, you will see that it has a great deal in common with monastic life. It's about people living together and doing it in order to help each other become more holy.

Accepting people as they are is perhaps one of the greatest things that came out of Vatican II. We can accept people as they are: Jewish, Christian, pagan. I can accept you for who you are. That is the deepest meaning of hospitality.

One of the other great values that many Benedictine monasteries have, and ours surely does, is the value of cleanliness and order in the house. It's an important aspect when you have a group of people living together.

I am planning to be around here — always. Living in this beautiful spot on the mountain, looking at the valley all around is an inspiring physical environment. Our community is a permanent one. We are able to help each other. We have physical security in knowing the community will always take care of us. It is a family-inspired institution. We are part of a community that serves people educationally and spiritually in an enthusiastic and dedicated life.

One can't pray in a vacuum. You need to know what is happening in the world. We have a great respect for laypeople, and our prayers go out to them as much as they go into the monastery. My work with Catholic Action was a wonderful education for me. Our whole effort there was to help people put life and religion together. In the minds of many people there is a valley that separates life and religion, and that doesn't seem to be getting any better. Maybe it's actually getting worse.

But I have hopes for the future. Personally, I hope that God will give me the health I need to continue with the work I'm doing for some years to come. I'm happy with it. For the community I hope that it can keep a real sense of prayer. We also need to share with laypeople. I hope we continue to find enough young monks to keep the monastery going. I hope the seminary continues to thrive for the sake of the church. But I have come to believe that you can only depend on a certain amount of planning. It's family life. It's not all in our hands.

For the future of the church, I hope we can involve the laity in promoting the good of the church. I feel we are ignoring single men and women in the church community. I think we need to do some serious theological thinking about what we can offer this growing group in our society.

Sister

MARMION MAIERS

Born 1924

Sister Marmion is a member of the Benedictine community at Mother of God Monastery in Watertown, South Dakota.

Mother of God Monastery is located on the outskirts of Watertown, a midsized town not far from the Minnesota state line. The monastery sits on a small hill and is quite a sight to see. Gleaming white with modern lines, it seems to hover in space. A pyramid-like central roof is flanked by two large side sections that are rounded at the ends, thus providing an abundance of light inside. Completed in 1997, it is a testament to the optimism of the sisters in Watertown. Sister Marmion, my elder at the monastery, is one of the "child" monastics I am meeting in my travels. She had joined the convent when she was only thirteen years old. Even though she is reaching eighty, she has a very youthful appearance. I know it is a foolish question, but at one point I can't resist: I ask her if she dyes her hair. With characteristic frankness she simply says no and continues our conversation.

Sister Marmion

MY FATHER DIED of cancer in 1930 at the beginning of the Depression and my mother had three girls and five boys to raise by herself. I had the privilege of attending Holy Cross School in Ipswich, South Dakota, for eight grades. For six of my years there I had Benedictine sisters as teachers. I was one of those little Catholic girls that always said she was going to be a sister, but I really didn't expect it to happen. Toward the end of my eighth grade, Sister Rosemarie, who became our first prioress here at Mother of God, was my teacher at the time and she said to me, "Alice, have you ever thought of going to the convent?" I told her that I had thought of it, but I did not think it would ever really happen. Well, I didn't know what to do. I was only thirteen years old, but she helped me. I filled out the forms and received my mother's consent, and in August of 1937, I was off to Sacred Heart Convent in Yankton, South Dakota.

When we talk about vocations today a variable to remember is that someone usually has to ask you, as Sister Rosemarie asked me, "Have you ever thought about going to the convent?" You may have a desire, but if no one ever asks, you may feel you are not worthy or not called. I think it takes someone to ask.

As a candidate for the sisterhood, I completed high school at the convent in three years. At the age of sixteen, in 1940, I was sent to Stephan Indian Mission in South Dakota. I had about forty little first- and second-graders to teach that year. Then, in June of 1940, I became a novice. I began to wonder at this time what I was missing in the outside world. Was I really being called? I left the convent at the age of seventeen and for three years I was "out in the world." For a year I worked in the kitchen at St. Luke's Hospital in Aberdeen, South Dakota. Then I worked in a candle factory in Ipswich for about a year. Then, in 1943, my older sister Margaret wanted to see what was out west. We took the bus to Portland, Oregon, with no particular destination in mind. We both got a job at Columbia Aircraft Company, where I worked in the office. When they closed, we found jobs in Seattle with Boeing. There I was a "Rosie the Rivet Bucker." But I did feel that the "hound of heaven" was pursing me, as I had a real urge to return to the convent. I did not say a word to my sister about my desire to return, and still, one day she turns to me and says, "When are you returning to the convent?" I wrote to Mother Jerome at Sacred Heart and asked her if I could return. She replied that she was just about to give my name, Sister Marmion, to a new novice, but she had decided to save it for me.

I returned in 1944, made first vows in 1946, and final vows in 1949. A few years ago, I celebrated my golden jubilee. I'm not sorry I entered when I was thirteen years old. I'm not sorry I left the convent for three years. I'm not sorry I returned. It was just meant to be. I have been enriched by all those experiences.

When I entered the convent at the age of thirteen, I had to fill out a form that stated what we would do in our vocation. I said that I wanted to be a nurse. I was at that age where nursing sounded romantic to me. Fortunately, the superior had the sense to realize that nursing was not where I belonged. Looking back now, I don't think I could stand being a nurse. The convent instead educated me as a teacher. I began teaching at the age of sixteen with just my high school education because that's what was done in those days. I would work on my college degree during the summers.

I spent the 1940s and 1950s teaching grade and junior high school. I spent many years at Stephan Indian Mission and at Richardton, North Dakota, but I also had teaching posts at Yankton and Dimock in South Dakota, and Lincoln, Nebraska. I finished my bachelor's degree at Mount Marty College in Yankton in 1958, and then completed my master's degree at the University of South Dakota in Vermillion in 1961. During the 1960s and 1970s, I was principal at a number of schools in both North and South Dakota. In the later 1970s, I became interested in family religious education, and I have spent much of the 1980s and 1990s doing pastoral religious education in a variety of parishes, and that is what I am still doing in Texarkana, Texas. I spend ten months of the year there, working half-time for the parish, and spend the other two months of the year back here at Mother of God Monastery.

I have enjoyed my life as a Benedictine. The only serious regrets I have had were early in my teaching career. I felt I was unjustly dealt with by some of my superiors in matters where I had no knowledge of wrongdoing. I was told that I might not be suited for the sisterhood, and I told them I was not sure I wanted to be so suited. But it was all temporary and straightened out. I'm happy that the "hound of heaven" I mentioned earlier kept after me. It follows Psalm 139 where it describes God pursuing us until we accept his presence and say, "Yes, I'm here."

The great joy of life has been my friendship with my fellow sisters. I have had much joy in our sense of community, doing things with the community — praying, playing cards, traveling, working alongside them. I'm not talking about short bursts of happiness, but long-term joyous living. I feel so blessed with their companionship.

Conversely I would have to say community life has also given me some sorrow. It is the flip side of the joy. Sometimes we have altercations, and there are times I have been hurt by comments or actions. The pain comes from the closeness.

My attitude toward the outside world has been shaped by having come to the convent at the age of thirteen, meaning I was raised in the routine. My life became methodical, and I have carried that over into my dealings on mission, my daily life, and my work. I do tend to get impatient with people who are not on time. I have lived by the bell at the monastery and then again with teaching school. Now I sometimes encounter adults in my parish work that are not very time conscious. It might be five minutes before a retreat is to begin and only one person has arrived. I sometimes have to grit my teeth.

When working in the outside world, I still try to schedule my work and activities around my prayer life. I will not lose contact with that monastic responsibility and pleasure.

The convent has shaped my morals and convictions and that extends to my outlook on the outside world. I am not swayed by popular beliefs. An example would be life issues. I try to have a consistent life ethic, whether dealing with abortion, capital punishment, suicide, or euthanasia. Life is valuable. God gave life and God can take away life.

While I learned the value of charity in the convent, I see so much wonderful charity among laypeople that it humbles me. With the commitment that I have made as a sister, I am expected to give of myself, but I see many remarkable laypeople giving so much of their time and energy. I don't think I do as much as they do.

We need to value others and treat them as such, and then our positive relationships will follow accordingly. When we do so, we work for the best interests of all. If we are truly concerned for others, all our values will fall in place. We will not do harmful things when we can prevent them. Giving of oneself always reaps so much more in return. God will not be outdone in generosity. I do think we need to acknowledge and value the good in people. A problem with my earlier years in the convent was that this was not done for fear of making one proud. We were corrected but rarely praised. We grew up with a low self-esteem. I had a very low self-esteem for many years. In more recent years we have been correcting this problem, and I now value myself.

As Benedictines our spiritual life flows around the Divine Office and Mass. We don't fit prayer around our work. We fit work around our prayer. Our life flows out from our prayer life. We also have *lectio,* spiritual reading, as part of our religious lives and growth. In the old days, we used to have one common reader, reading the same book to all of us. But now, and for some time, we have had the privilege of selecting our own *lectio,* and we do reading and meditating on our own.

Our special charism is hospitality. It is the Benedictine way. And hospitality is simply treating each other as Christ. Our communal prayer has Christ at its center with the Eucharist as the focal point. Jesus comes to us as body and blood. It is the core of faith. I must admit that sometimes it can become a bit routine and I don't appreciate the miracle, and I have to bring myself back to the mystery and wonder of the experience.

I value the way the pace of the day is structured by our prayer. Without it our lives would be arid. Some people on the outside might see all this prayer as a waste of time, but it is not. We are not just praying for ourselves; it is not selfish. We are praying for all people. It is not an easy life.

The Rule of St. Benedict is the foundation for our life of prayer and work. I do like Chapter 72, about the good zeal of monastics. I think it says in a nutshell what the life of Benedictines should be: to compete with a holy zeal to do good to one another.

One of the exercises we did as novices was to go through the Holy Rule and find every reference we could to charity. It was a huge number because that is what our life is about—charity and love. It comes down to Matthew's chapter 25: "Truly I tell you: anything you did for one of my brothers here, however insignificant, you did for me." It is not about how much time we spend on our knees. It is how we treat our fellow human beings that matters now and will matter in the end. I think that is what Benedict is saying with the good zeal of the monastic: treat others as Christ. It always comes back to that for me.

We always read Chapter 49 just before Lent. It encourages us to try to do what we normally do but more perfectly. It is such good advice for any time, not just Lent.

And finally, the very first word of the Rule: "Listen." We are always in a learning mode. We never know it all. Listening is so important. We need to be aware of others and include them, whether it's a discussion or anything else. We need to be inclusive.

Our spiritual life paces our physical life. In the early days, we focused on the Benedictine *ora et labora,* prayer and work, and we didn't pay much attention to a third consideration, leisure. We did have a scheduled recreation period where we would sew or play cards or games. I loved playing cards. Today we have much more self-determination. If we have a regular job, it determines our schedule.

The care of our physical bodies is guided by Benedictine concern. I have had a series of problems with my knees and legs, and the care has always been first-class. We are looked after with loving care in our family spirit.

As I mentioned, most of the year I live with two other Benedictine sisters in Texarkana. They are my family, and we have a loving family spirit. We divide the work among us and share the cleaning, cooking, and shopping duties. I treasure our Benedictine love. In our Benedictine life we are so blessed. I think of the hundredfold blessings Jesus promised the apostles; we receive more than that in our lives in the here and now.

I do have hopes for the future. My hopes are that we will attract new members so we can continue the monastic life. To do so, I think the composition of our community may change more in the future than it has in the past. We have a summer volunteer program for women and men who are evaluated and matched for work that is needed. They form an extended membership. We also have our oblate organization, like most Benedictine communities; and we have lay associates, both women and men, who live, work, and pray with us for a full year.

I hope we will get more permanent members, but I also hope we continue to nurture this extended family of the monastery that commits for shorter times. It is a blessing for them and a blessing for us. We are enriched by all who come into contact with us.

Father

THEODORE HECK

Born 1901

Father Theodore is a member of the Benedictine community at St. Meinrad Archabbey in St. Meinrad, Indiana.

❁

When the abbot of St. Meinrad first wrote me that their elder for my meeting would be a priest born back in 1901, I had some reservations. I was concerned that communication might not be too fluid with a man so advanced in years, but I did not want to argue with the abbot of one of the most esteemed abbeys in the country.

My concerns are quickly laid to rest at our first meeting: Father Theodore has a stack of notes he has prepared for each question I want to ask him. He is fully organized, and his clarity of thought puts me to shame. When we talk about how he has been using his time in recent years he says, "I have set myself up with a reading program where I read so much history, so much science, so much religion a day. To date, I have read 1,956 books. I write a little summary of each book and keep it in my records." I am speechless, realizing I have met my ultimate role model, someone who gives true meaning to the much-used phrase "lifelong learner."

Father Theodore has continued to surprise me in the years since our first meeting. Recently I was eating lunch with two monks from St. Meinrad who were visiting Blue Cloud Abbey. I asked about Father Theodore's health and the response was, "Oh, he's just fine. He's learning how to use the Internet." Every time I write him, he sends back a neatly handwritten note inquiring about my well-being.

Father Theodore

I CAME TO St. Meinrad in 1918 with the intention of studying to be a priest. While I was studying at St. Meinrad seminary, I read a biography of St. Benedict and was very intrigued. I also witnessed the spiritual life and work of the Benedictine monks here, and I gradually became interested in a Benedictine vocation for myself along with the priesthood. There were also other students studying at the seminary who were drawn to the Benedictines, and that also helped to encourage me. The Benedictine way of living was appealing to me. The group praying of the Divine Office seemed to me a wonderful way to praise God. In the Office we have a constant contact with God, and he is talking to us through our prayer. The Lord says, "When two or three are gathered in my name I am with them." The impression of spiritual growth, the fuller service to God in talent and way of life led me to seek through prayer and example the Benedictine way and a wholesome life. I grew up in a very religious family. Two of my younger sisters also joined a religious order.

I entered the novitiate in 1922, took my first vows in 1923, final vows in 1926, and was ordained a priest in 1929. In addition to living the monastic life within the community, for which I am deeply grateful, I have devoted my life to the assignments of teaching, administration, guidance, and parish administration and assistance. After completing my studies in college and theology for the priesthood, I was privileged to take advanced studies at the Catholic University of America in Washington, D.C. I spent three years there and received a master's and doctorate in administration.

Here at St. Meinrad I taught courses in education, mathematics, and social studies in the college and school of theology. I served as rector of the school of theology for ten years and dean of the school for seventeen years. I developed a program of teacher education for the seminarians, preparing them for their license to teach in Catholic high schools. I served as president of the American Benedictine Academy for six years, and I have provided parochial assistance for an extended period while living at the monastery.

In community service, I was appointed subprior and later prior of St. Meinrad Archabbey. Excluding my years away for graduate studies, my teaching assignments here at St. Meinrad extended from 1929 to 1987.

In 1987, I quit teaching, but I haven't quit learning. I still help students and also help occasionally in parishes and the infirmary.

❁

The fact that I am a priest and can offer the Holy Sacrifice of the Mass is my greatest joy. I appreciate that more than anything else. To carry this out in a community of faith-loving members adds to its significance. To me community means all the people, and I include them all in my prayers and works of service. It has been a joy for me to be a Benedictine monk. That sounds a bit elevated, but it's true. I thank God daily for the vocation that I have. It is a wonderful way of life. Maybe when I was younger I would have fished around a bit more, but when I look back, I am glad I took this path. Even the difficult days had a silver lining. I appreciate it all the more when I look back at the opportunities and problems that have been part of my life. I see how they have been solved, and I am thankful more and more for my monastic life.

When I think about it, I have not had a deep sorrow in my life. The death of relatives and confreres brings grief, but there is always the hope of eternal life toward which we are all striving. It is a sorrow that religion does not seem to have a hold on many people today. They don't have guidance to form ideals. They are trying to live a life without the guidelines that religion can provide. People who have abused their lives, morally or physically, cause me sorrow, but prayer and the mercy of God bring hope.

Our monastery serves as a great safeguard for our spiritual lives and happiness. Some people think we are all walled up here and can't do anything, but that certainly isn't the case. The ideals we have are high enough to keep us interested and busy. Compared with other people, I think we are very fortunate. I remember my mother used to say that we children were very fortunate in our family life. I feel the same way for the family life of the monastery.

My parents were good Christians and emphasized Christian service. They required that service of their children as well. My background prepared me for the Benedictine way of life. We had a wonderful home life. Well, in those days you had a bicycle or a horse and you couldn't go too far. We all had chores and we were committed to them and to the family. We had a little farm with cows, horses, and chickens. There were plenty of chores to do. I found that coming from a large family, three brothers and three sisters, was a good foundation for communal living.

My Benedictine spiritualism grew through my years as a student but was really established when I became a novice. It has enlarged and matured over the years. The community life, the Divine Office in choir, the daily participation in Mass all appeal to me. I am also drawn to the Christian life and various forms of service practiced by Benedictines: teaching, parish work, and missions.

Our lives are in order here. We have our communal meals, we have an infirmary and all the medical care we need, we have our abbot to give us spiritual instruction, we have our own duties within the community. All these things give us a way of living. It grows as time goes on. It may seem as if we are repeating the same thing over and over, but in truth it is a constant program of growth. I enjoy reading and try to keep up in the fields of religion, history, the sciences, and local matters. It's a way to keep your mind growing. I have read a good bit of Benedictine history. I have spent nearly all my religious life in the monastery and have appreciated the wisdom of the Benedictine Rule and its application to the local monastery. To me, this life is an ideal way of living for the service of God and for preparation for eternity.

There are two parts of the Rule that are very special for me, the Prologue and Chapter 73, the end. The Prologue sets the structure for the entire Rule, and Chapter 73 is the conclusion that brings it all together. Benedict writes in the conclusion, "The reason we have written this rule is that, by observing it in monasteries, we can show that we have some degree of virtue and the beginnings of monastic life." Later he goes on to say, "Are you hastening toward your heavenly home? Then with Christ's help, keep this little rule that we have written for beginners."

The Rule teaches us that respect for life and social justice are very important values that apply to humankind. Religion as a service to humankind, and our duty toward God, find many opportunities that are carried out in religious life. I feel that the Benedictine Rule provides guidelines for both religious and laity to lead us to the goal for which we were created — to know, love, and serve God and our fellow people. To serve God and your neighbor is basic. If your life doesn't fill those needs, you have missed the boat.

The Rule defines our values very clearly even though it was written fifteen hundred years ago. Every three years the abbots come together and revise our constitution, which is our modern interpretation of the Rule. This makes the Rule a living document in our times. The Rule also stresses the value of manual work, and I think that is still very important today. We need to respect all people's value, their skills, and contributions to the community.

Considering the spiritual life as a major factor in life on earth, I have used its principles as guiding points in my attitude in viewing the outside world and feel that the church and its doctrines make a difference wherever they are put into practice. They are a goal toward which we should constantly strive. Charity and justice are important goals to try to achieve. Here at the monastery we have tried to benefit the outside world around us. In earlier days we had a farming operation, and we worked with farmers around us to try to help improve agriculture and rural life. Times have changed since I came here. I came up a dirt road in a buggy pulled by a horse. We no longer have the large garden of my early years, but we have resumed gardening on a smaller scale.

Now that I am in the later days of life, my hopes are primarily spiritual, accepting God's will for the future. God has blessed me in many ways. My hope is that I can thank God as I should.

The monastery has recently gone through a long period of working on building and renovation development. My hopes are that we can now focus our efforts on spiritual and intellectual development. There is also some increased interest among young people and older people about the religious life, and that also gives me hope. There seems to be more interest now from people in their thirties, forties, and even fifties in a religious vocation.

Sister

LEONETTE HOESING

Born 1915

Sister Leonette is a member of the Benedictine community at Sacred Heart Monastery in Yankton, South Dakota.

Sacred Heart Monastery is perched on a cliff overlooking the Missouri River. Below it the river turns and twists like a giant snake, making its way through rolling hills. Sister Leonette is a living part of the river and the hills. Born and raised within range of the bells of the monastery, she is an indigenous sister, one with a lifelong affinity and attachment to the place and its people. Some people on the "outside" think of monastic life as an austere, solemn existence. Sister Leonette is a wonderful example to the contrary. Bursting with energy, she describes the joys of her life: "The greatest happiness comes in the times we spend together. Every year we do a Mardi Gras celebration that is much fun. We need some occasions that we can do downright stupid things to give us the strength for our other work. This year we did an Olympic theme. Each of our small groups living together formed an Olympic team and created a theme for their group. My, we were a sight. It really brings out the creativity of the sisters." She has photographs to back up her assertion, and they really are quite a sight.

Sister Leonette

I COME FROM a large family of ten children. Growing up very poor during the Depression, we learned how to share, and we developed a real sense of community in the family. We learned to make do with very little. I remember my mother taking the barley and roasting it, and that was our coffee. We were always happy as children. We made our own entertainment and toys. Anything could become toys, even corncobs. We never realized we were poor, because everyone else in the area was in the same shape. I grew up on a farm not far from here. My first three school years were at public school, but then, even in those terrible years, the parishioners managed to build a Catholic school, and I had the Benedictine sisters from Sacred Heart Monastery as my teachers. My Benedictine influence began with them. I also had an aunt who was a Benedictine sister in Minnesota who would come and visit. But I don't think I ever really thought of becoming a Benedictine until one time in the tenth grade we were asked what we wanted to do when we got out of school. I had thought I might like to be a sister, but I knew if I wrote that down all the kids would laugh at me, so I put down a "sister nurse" so if they asked me I could say I wanted to be a nurse. I didn't give it much more thought after that and the sisters did not pester me, and I was grateful for that.

The Catholic school ended in the tenth grade, and my father wanted me to continue with a Catholic education at Mount Marty, the school connected to Sacred Heart, but we were so poor I didn't see how I could. I did end up going and worked for part of my board, but that year was a terrible year on the farm and I knew I couldn't stay at Mount Marty for a second year. I'm sure we didn't ever pay the bill for the first year, and I know the sisters never asked us for it. I told my dad I would stay home and help with the farm. My father cared so much for me and wanted so much for me, so I was somewhat afraid to tell him that I wanted to become a sister. I decided to wait until one evening when he was driving me home from choir practice. It was dark and he couldn't see me, and I couldn't see him. I kept putting it off and putting it off and finally we were in the total dark of the garage and I told him. First he was quiet, and then he said that he would never stand in the way of anything I wanted.

I did stay home and helped on the farm for two years, and then entered Sacred Heart Monastery. I was able to go back to Mount Marty and finish high school. During the time I was back home I often longed for Mount Marty, especially on days when the wind was in the right direction and we could hear the monastery bells. I did find it difficult to leave home, since I was the oldest and I felt some responsibility to my family. I had originally thought that I might like to do mission work, but my Benedictine aunt told me that one didn't need to go to Africa to do mission work, as there was plenty to do right here. I took my first vows in 1935 and my solemn vows in 1940.

I began by teaching for thirteen years. I taught the upper grades, and those were the days when we had four grades in one room. I'm not sure how we did it. We also taught music, took care of the church, and did the janitorial work. We did everything. I remember one school in Lincoln, Nebraska. We arrived in August and the school hadn't been used in twelve years. The windows were knocked out and the entire school was a mess. We remodeled it, and we were determined not to start school until everything was in tip-top shape. We had so much fun. Of course we were young and foolish at that time.

Those were some of the happiest years of my life. I taught in many different mission schools around the region.

After that I worked with the formation program here at Sacred Heart. I worked with the novices for fifteen years and at the same time oversaw the choir. I loved the chant. It was a real spiritual formation in my life.

In 1961, I became subprioress for four years, then I was called to Victoria, British Columbia, to be prioress there at St. Mary's Priory. I was at St. Mary's for twelve years. We were helping a very needy community there. It was a difficult time but a time of great growth for me. I had the privilege of working with a young bishop who had just come from Vatican II, and I really learned where the church was going. It was most enriching. I was able to work with people of many faiths. The primary work of the sisters there was the care of the elderly. They had two hundred patients, and they worked hard to take care of these people whom no one else would look after. They worked with such kindness. Before I returned to Yankton, I studied at Seattle University and received my master's degree in religious education.

I came back here in 1978. In 1980, I became oblate director, which I have been ever since. The oblates have been growing by leaps and bounds. Sometimes I feel that even if there isn't a great deal of growth in the vocations of the monastery, there will still be a broadening of Benedictine influence in the community through the oblates. There is much in the Rule that is so right for family living.

❁

As a young sister, before I took my solemn vows, I would hear the sisters talking about the spirit of Benedict. It bothered me because I didn't know what it was. I would ask people, but they never could tell me what it really was. I felt that if I didn't come to an understanding of this spirit I couldn't make my solemn vows. Then we had a retreat given by a young priest from Latrobe. He began the retreat by saying that because everyone understood the spirit of Benedict, he didn't need to deal with that. I just wanted to scream! But then he did go on to explain the spirit in simple terms, which is to present Christ to the age in which you live. That hit me so hard. I'm still not sure I know all it means, but it was a sentence that I could really hold on to, and it has become the guide for my life: to present Christ to the age in which you live. It has been a strong guidance for me, especially in all the years of change when we changed our habit, the chant, and so many other things. Through all those changes I hung on to the fact that we are to present Christ to the age in which we live. Christ doesn't change, and all these other changes do not touch me. No matter what situation I find myself in, that sentence has been a help. I may not know what it means fully, but I keep trying. That one sentence has been my guiding light. When I taught my novices, I tried to make sure they had some understanding of the spirit of Benedict.

The Divine Office for me has always been my love; the corporate worship of the sisters has meant everything to me.

The key for me has been balance. I have always found the Rule to be very balanced. The Rule is really not a rule but a way of living. At its heart is everyday living as best as you can — with all your mistakes and foibles but trying to live the ordinary in an extraordinary way. The Benedictine life presents you with both the joys and the sorrows that come with community living. Such a life has the built-in factor of knowing that, when things get out of balance, it is not healthy and needs correction. There is balance in our lives, in our prayers, the food we eat, our exercise and our sleep, and everything else we do.

The Rule is an expansive document without borders. St. Benedict seems to have caught the universe with this vision of life. While the essence of the Rule never changes, the outside aspects of it adapt to fit any situation, and always in a way that points us to Christ. Benedict always points us to Christ, not to the Rule but to Christ. I have so many favorite parts of the Rule: the wonderful Prologue; Chapter 72 (I used to make the novices memorize the whole chapter); Chapter 53; and all the first seven chapters to which I come back time and time again. This year during Lent our prioress instructed us to read the Rule through twice, cover to cover, without a commentary. Then we were to contemplate which parts brought us peace and which parts we might need to work on. It was a wonderful experience.

The Rule teaches us reverence, and it has made me understand that there isn't an inside world and an outside world, *everything* is holy. Everything is to be treated with reverence, whether it is the things I use or nature around me. I remember at my last teaching job we sanded down and varnished every desktop. There was not one scratch to be found anywhere, because if there is even one scratch the kids are tempted to put their own marks on it. I used to tell them that their desks and even their pencils are sacred. I told them that St. Benedict taught that we should treat everything like the holy chalice. They could understand that and they could remember it. I'm sure it helped some of them in their own homes. That kind of reverence can be used anywhere.

St. Benedict should be the patron saint of our entire environmental system. If we treated our world with the reverence he asked for, we would not have today's problems. We would not have poverty, we would not have wars or a degraded ecosystem.

We need to work for beauty, even in small places, in our homes, in our yards, wherever we can create and recognize it. It all comes down to reverence for things and especially people. The world becomes sacred to me through the Rule and gospel living. That's what the Rule is: gospel living.

❁

I've had so many joys from so many things. I would have to say that community has been my greatest joy, working together and being able to build a community that can reach out to others. My blood family has given me great joy, and also the many friends I have had over the years. All my brothers and sisters live within a fifty-mile radius of here. Twice a year we all get together and we have so much fun. We eat, play, and sing together. We are very close to one another.

I'm so grateful to my community. They have given me much. I was just a simple little farm girl and now I've been to Rome twice and even to the Holy Land.

My life has been so rich and full that I am eternally grateful. I have had so many opportunities given to me by this life. Coming here when I was seventeen years old, I have spent my life here. I can think of no regrets, but certainly I have had sorrows in my life, everyone does. There have been difficult changes to get through, but they have been stepping-stones to a greater fullness of life. I have been so blessed and fortunate. Even now I wish I could do more to pay back a little of my blessings. I wish I could do more to help the poor and disadvantaged. To see the suffering in the world and the inhumanity that some people must bear brings me sorrow. The lack of Christian love and reverence for one another and for the planet by individuals and corporations is also a sadness for me. It's also a sorrow to see that many people do not have the opportunity for a good education. Many times this lack of opportunity comes about from the greed of others; inequality is a sorrow.

At Sacred Heart we have tried to emphasize three basic values in our mission work. First, an awareness of God: seeking God in our prayer and savoring the word of Scripture, listening for the divine voice in the stillness of our own hearts, regarding the ordinary with reverence in our work, our prayer. The second value is that of community: building trustful and loving relationships with God, one another, and the earth; striving to give and receive in balance for the good of the whole; being there for others as they are for us; learning the daily art of forgiveness and peacemaking; and sharing our worship, our table, our times of joy, and our times of sadness. The third primary value for our monastery is hospitality: to welcome all as Christ, to share our gifts with others, and to open our hearts and doors to those pushed to the edges of life.

We need more awareness of the injustices around us. Even in our own town there are people in need. The community has started having a banquet once a week for anyone who needs it. It is a free meal for anyone who would like to come, for whatever need they might have, the need of a meal or the need of companionship. We often have nearly two hundred people. They started it about a year ago, and every week another community group or business sponsors the event and takes care of the meal. It's an example of people starting to care for others.

My hope for the future of the church is that we can all come together and sit at one table. I hope we can learn to respect each other in our various faiths. No one has all the answers. We need to work with a sense of openness—like Jesus.

For our monastery, I hope we continue to have wonderful young women joining us. We have some fine young people with great possibilities. We need even more. We know that the future of the community will not be what it is now. We know things will change, but we have faith that what will evolve will be okay. Who knows, in twenty-five years it may be that not everyone in the community will make permanent vows. There may be people who are called here for a period of time and then leave. That has happened before, when in the sixties we had people leave. But I look out and see what wonderful things they have done in their communities. They are still spreading our work. In the future there will still be some who want to make a permanent commitment, but probably not all. We certainly don't know what will happen in the future, but that is one possibility.

——— Father ———

BEDE STOCKER

Born 1916

Father Bede is a member of the Benedictine community at Marmion Abbey in Aurora, Illinois.

Marmion Abbey is located in a far west suburb of Chicago. While it is well known for its Marmion Academy for Boys, I am not here to speak to one of its current academics or a distinguished past abbot. I am here to meet Father Bede, the "Christmas tree monk." Father Bede's face has the texture of well-weathered leather, the type of skin I have seen so often on the faces of elder farmers on the plains of South Dakota. His long years of tending and nurturing spruce trees for holiday sales have left their wear and tear on his skin and his joints. But it is obvious from our conversation that there is nowhere in this world he would rather be than out there tending his trees. Soon I come to realize that I am talking to a remarkably honest person. At one point in our discussion about Benedictine prayer life he says, "I confess, I have always had trouble keeping concentration. I do the Office and enjoy it and I'm glad I'm there, but sometimes when the Office is finished, I wonder where my mind was all that time." This comment is typical of the absolute openness and humility of Father Bede, a monk who worships as much with the work of his hands as with the prayers of his mouth.

Father Bede

BACK IN OUR DAY we went to seminary right out of grade school (eighth grade), and I wanted to be a priest. I went to St. Meinrad to study to be a priest. My dad had a grocery store, and he was going to pay the tuition. But the Depression hit, and Dad couldn't afford the three hundred dollars a year for tuition and board. The rector of the seminary said that if I was thinking about possibly being a Benedictine, they would pay my expenses. I thought about it during midterm retreat and decided to do it. After my fourth year of high school, I almost didn't come back to the seminary. There was a good-looking girl who had caught my eye. But I did come back and in the fifth year the Lord took care of me. It was my best year ever. I decided definitely to become a Benedictine at that time. It was also at this time that I read the *Autobiography of St. Therese of Lisieux.* It was and still is inspiring for me. It helped give me the strength to strive for the love of God, which is what the Benedictine life is all about. It has been said that people come to a monastery for many reasons but stay for only one—the love of God. I had no problem with the vocation after that.

I was ordained in 1942 and during that year, while finishing my fourth year of theology, I also worked in St. Meinrad's printing office. In 1943, I was appointed assistant at the parish in Ferdinand, Indiana. After a short time there, I was reassigned to the printing office, and was there until 1947, when I was assigned with twelve other monks of St. Meinrad to serve here at Marmion. Originally a daughter house of St. Meinrad, Marmion was later elevated to the status of an independent abbey. We had been given the chance to express our preference either to stay at St. Meinrad or to go to

Marmion. I said I was willing to go if sent. I was sent. I was designated the novice master here from 1947 to 1965. During that time, I was also teaching at the high school. I taught religion and some Latin and English. Both then and now, I help with parish work in the area, saying Mass nearly every Sunday at some parish church.

In 1970, I inherited the job of taking care of our Christmas tree farm, and I'm still at it. Father Andrew is now my helper and does all the big jobs with machinery and so on. He works harder than I do. We plant about ten thousand trees a year. It takes between six and ten years before they are ready to harvest. It's quite a job with all the trimming and straightening. I have a crew of students that I supervise in the summer, which is quite a job as well. We sell about seven thousand trees a year. People come out and pick their own from the fields. One of my hobbies is carving wooden napkins rings, a hobby I began years ago while waiting for the tree hunters in the Christmas tree season. I've carved a napkin ring for every monk in the community. Another hobby I have is repairing old clocks. I also take care of our orchard.

Someone asked me a couple of days ago when I was going to retire. I told them that if I had to sit down I would be dead next week. I'm used to working. My mother's maiden name was Bauerle. It means "little farmer" in German. I've been trying to live up to that all my life.

I have absolutely no regrets in having chosen a Benedictine life. I just wish I'd done better. My life has been one of continual joy and peace with the community. The day I took my vows and the day of my ordination were a special part of that continual joy — the joy of realizing the privilege of living with dedicated men.

Well, I do enjoy playing cards and winning too. I do grumble when I don't get good cards all evening. Benedict has some hard things to say about grumbling.

Our lives here are lives of *ora et labora. Ora* for Benedict's seeking of God in prayer. The Divine Office is the heart of the Benedictine prayer life. *Labora* for the necessary manual labor and chores around the monastery. I'm inclined toward the *labora* side. We need to have both the scholars and the laborers at the monastery, and I fit more with the laborers.

I've got good health and also a new knee that's working pretty well. I live a regular kind of life. My daily schedule is usually as follows: I rise at 5:45 in the morning; Divine Office is at 6:30 a.m.; 6:45 — meditation; 7:15 — breakfast; at 8:30 a.m., I take care of various chores, then I go out to work on the trees; at 11:00 a.m., I come back in to change and clean up for Mass; 11:30, we have Mass, followed by lunch at 12 noon; 12:30 p.m. — nap; at 1:15, I am back out to work on the trees, or I do other jobs; at 4 p.m., I come back in and clean up for prayer; 4:30 p.m. — *lectio* reading; 5:00 p.m. — Divine Office; 5:30 — supper; at 6:00 p.m., I watch the TV news; 6:30 — Divine Office; 7:00 p.m. — recreation, playing cards, letter writings, reading, etc.; then I go to bed around 10:30 to 11:00 p.m.

It's a healthy life. St. Paul says that everything is a grace. I've often thought about what he meant by that, and I think it is true that everything is a grace. The Lord takes care of all, and I take what comes. Monastic life teaches you that.

I believe the most important value the world needs to appreciate and make use of is real family life. Monastic life gives a good example of this: monks pray together, share meals together, recreate together, and each one takes his share of the work of the monastery. I remember writing to my folks as a young man, trying to explain our life in the monastery. The best I could do was to say we are like a family, with each member using his distinct abilities to help the whole community.

The spiritual element in our life is, of course, the most important. We need to remember the mystery of salvation. Our Lord came down to save us. St. John says, "He loved us so much He sent His own Son to us." We need to realize that love and to live in that love. During the day we all need to talk to God. He loves each one of us, and we need to return that love. That love needs to soak into our lives.

We need to rush and worry less. We need to take the time to experience the love of God and appreciate what we have.

I appreciate very much the sacrifices people make who make their vocation in the "outside" world. For instance, to fulfill duties as parents is not an easy task. There is the financial burden of paying bills, taxes, and so on, whereas we individual monks do not have such worries. One of the monks is assigned treasurer, and his duties include balancing the budget and paying the bills. All our basic needs are cared for. I especially appreciate the big job parents have in raising children in today's world.

People in the "outside" world may also wonder and worry about what will happen when they encounter old age or sickness. That is no worry for us. We can be quite certain that our fellow monks will be there to care for us.

The Rule of St. Benedict is our guide in many matters. As a former novice master, I relate to Chapter 5 on obedience and Chapter 7 on humility. I think they really summarize St. Benedict's spirituality. This emphasis on humility and obedience became more difficult to get across in the 1960s when the individualism of the times was so strong, but I didn't give in on those points. After so many years as novice master, it was a sorrow to see good men leave the monastery in the late 1960s. Most received permission, but two left without permission. It was a sorrow to see these men with problems and not at peace. Our Lord said in the gospels that we were to learn of him in being meek and humble of heart. He didn't say learn how to do miracles, but learn to be humble and obedient.

I also like the chapter on the abbot. It's really marvelous—the way it says the abbot shouldn't be too suspicious or overanxious. That goes for everybody. Dads and moms shouldn't be too suspicious or overanxious about their kids either, or a husband about a wife or a wife about a husband. It fits everybody. There are so many things in the Rule that extend far beyond monastic life. Benedict was such a wise man. But the Rule isn't all original. He used a lot of information from previous sources, especially the Scriptures and particularly the Psalms. In his day the monks had to memorize all the Psalms. I don't even know what a lot of the Psalms mean even when I read them in English.

I have hopes for the future. I hope the Lord will give our pope a long life. I hope our monastery keeps up its good work and our school maintains its good reputation. I also hope that the boys who attend our school can become more spiritually minded rather than just focused on material success.

For the monastery I hope we continue to have a good number of vocations. We have five new novices coming in, and I hope they will be successful.

Sister

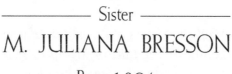

M. JULIANA BRESSON

Born 1904

Sister Juliana is a member of the Benedictine Sisters of Perpetual Adoration in Clyde, Missouri.

The monastery of the Sisters of Perpetual Adoration is tucked away in the gently rolling hills of Missouri. It is a stately structure that projects a feeling of a time long past. On the morning of our departure, the prioress invites Sammy and me to join her and Sister Juliana for a private breakfast. After breakfast our conversation shifts to driving directions. The prioress is giving us detailed instructions on how to find our way to the main highway. She tells us to turn right here, then left, then right and then left again. At that point Sister Juliana quietly interjects that a right-hand turn, not a left-hand turn, is needed at that specific point. The prioress looks at the near centenarian who has never driven a car, and says, "No, it is a left turn." We leave it at that, but five or ten minutes later the prioress stops in mid-sentence and says, "Wait, Sister Juliana is correct. You do *make a right-hand turn at that corner." What an inspiring way to end our time with this remarkable woman who quietly dedicated her life with so much clarity to God and to her community.*

Sister Juliana

WHEN I WAS about six years old, I would see Catholic sisters once a year when they would come to our town begging for funds for their school. For some reason they fascinated me, and I said I wanted to be one when I grew up. My little sister and I would put towels on our heads and dress up like nuns and pray, since that was what we thought nuns did. But the next day we would play house with our dolls, and then the next day we would be nuns again.

When I was fifteen I began seriously thinking about becoming a nun. My mother and I went to Cleveland and we visited two communities, but I wasn't at all attracted to either. They were both teaching communities, and I did not want to be a teacher and I did not want to be a nurse. I didn't know where else to look. Our family subscribed to the publication *Tabernacle and Purgatory,* which was published here at Clyde. In many of the issues they had articles inviting girls to inquire about vocations. The problem was Clyde was eight hundred miles from where we lived. I had two older cousins who were going to Clyde to possibly join, and I persuaded my mother to let me go along. We came and stayed about a week. When I got home from the long train ride, my mother put me to bed in her room that was shaded by a big elm tree and was cooler than my room. She came in and sat beside me and I said, "Mom, Clyde is where I want to be." It was settled right there. I entered on October 1, 1920 — eight hundred miles from home. I was sixteen years old. My two cousins joined a teaching order in Cleveland.

When I first arrived, I was so young they sent me to their boarding school where I studied for a few months; then they sent me to the printery. At that time we were using foundry type. You set one letter at a time. For six years I used that method. Then we received a machine similar to a Linotype, called an Intertype. I learned that typesetting process and operated that machine for over eighteen years. Then I was receptionist at the monastery for four years, then back to the printery, then I took care of the sacristy for two years, then back to the printery again. They always wanted me back at the printery. We had that Intertype machine for forty-seven years. When we had to have it fixed, the repair people could not believe that we were still using it. I would tell them that we knew how to take care of a machine. It's like a human—keep it well oiled, cleaned, and it will operate. If you don't feed a human and give him rest, he won't operate. We took good care of all our machines.

I remember once when we were having trouble, I took the whole ninety-key keyboard apart. Each key had five parts, as the machine was very complicated. The supervising sister at that time didn't think I should do it. But I thought I could. I took every key apart and had all the parts strung out on three tables. The supervisor was so nervous she wouldn't come in the room. She was sure we would have to bring in a mechanic to put it back together. But I got it all back together and it worked, and later I took it apart a second time.

When the old Intertype finally gave out, we went with an IBM cold-type system. I learned this new typesetting system in 1972 and ran it for nine years. I went from handsetting metal type to IBM electronic typesetting in my work. When they transferred the magazine publishing to our monastery in Tucson, I volunteered to go down and typeset on the new computers, but believe it or not, they turned me down.

I was in our Kansas City house for two years, 1944 to 1945, serving as sacristan. In 1945, I was called back to Clyde to serve as receptionist and also helped to organize the library; then, in 1956, I took over the library. In 1963, I was sent to our house in San Diego where I redid their library. I then returned to Clyde in 1971 and worked with the printery and the library. In 1986, the new superior decided I needed to retire, but the new librarian needed some help, and I'm still assistant librarian here. I'm still going pretty strong.

My most joyful day as a Benedictine was the one when they accepted me into the community. I enjoyed my vocation as a sister and adorer. And I've always taken an interest in my work. I enjoyed the printery. My father was a mechanic, and I guess I took to it naturally. I love books, and I love to read. They say that working in a library is an education, and that's where I achieved most of my education. I have no regrets about having chosen a monastic life. I would not exchange my vocation for another.

One of my favorite parts of the Rule of St. Benedict is Chapter 7 and the first stage of humility. St. Benedict says we need to live in the presence of God. Another of my favorite chapters is Chapter 72, where Benedict says to prefer nothing to Christ. And in between those two, in Chapter 58 he tells the novice master to be certain that the novice truly seeks God. There you have it. With those three points you have the foundation of your spiritual life.

Benedict envisioned his monks living secluded lives. He believed that the monastery should be self-contained. Our Swiss founders in the nineteenth century wanted to open a convent of perpetual adoration where they would spend their lives in prayer adoring the Blessed Sacrament. The authorities at that time were not open to the idea of a new order, but they allowed the sisters to become established when they started a school for poor girls as a kind of front for their real intentions. Our founding sisters came from Switzerland in 1874. They set up here in Missouri to be near Conception Abbey. They had a school and began their perpetual adoration of the Blessed Sacrament on March 28, 1878. That means they were adorers and had prayer before the Blessed Sacrament day and night. That is the purpose for which we were founded here.

St. Benedict saw his monks living lives of prayer. The perpetual adoration dovetails with this. We succeeded each other in prayer before the Blessed Sacrament, hour after hour, day and night. This was maintained until 1986 when it was decided that each sister would keep her hour of adoration privately and according to how her work permitted. We each also maintain an hour of *lectio,* prayerful reading.

We also pray the Divine Office daily. For forty-eighty years I prayed the Office in Latin. Then in 1968, after Vatican II, we gradually changed to English. We also shortened the time. We now pray the cycle of the 150 Psalms in four weeks. We used to pray the cycle in two weeks. We spend a total of about two and a half hours a day praying the Office. In our vocation we need to be faithful to our prayer life. We need to be honest to our *lectio.* Prayer is our life. Prayer is to God. We pray firstly to praise, honor, and worship God. Secondly, in prayer we aspire to union with God.

Even when we were doing the night adoration, provisions were made to be sure we got enough rest to stay healthy. We always had adequate medical care, and since Vatican II we have more choice in our care. We have a good infirmary here, and we have a major health-care center in St. Louis where we have first-class care and full-time nurses.

Our schedule structured our life and gave it regularity. We had plain, substantial meals. We were permitted coffee breaks mid-mornings and mid-afternoons. We had our own farm and bought very little outside the monastery. We had a huge kitchen garden, we had our own beef, we had up to two thousand chickens, and we had a renowned, prize-winning dairy herd. We even sent one bull to the pope's herd in Italy. We always tried to be a self-sustaining community, not depending on outside donations.

There have been difficult times. When my brother Charles was ordained a priest and I was not allowed to attend his first Mass, that was very hard. My family thought it was a crime that I wasn't allowed to come, but it was the custom at the time. Others made the same sacrifice. The death of my siblings, some in their sixties, was very difficult. My family is all gone now. It was hard not being able to go help them when they were ill. Nowadays a sister is permitted to go home and help her family when the need arises. Vatican II has been a blessing. When I first joined not even our mail was private. It was all read going out and coming in. Now I can put a stamp on my letter, seal it, and send it out. We are now allowed to go out of the monastery. Up until Vatican II the only time I stepped off the premises was to go to the doctor or the dentist. We can now visit our families. After coming to the convent I never saw my parents' home again. My first trip to my family was in 1968, forty-eight years after joining the convent, when I took my first vacation with my family. In 1971 I went to Niagara Falls with my brothers and sisters. It would have been my parents' seventieth wedding anniversary. They had honeymooned at the Falls in 1901. I also went to Rome and the Holy Land. My brothers sacrificed to give me that trip as a gift for my golden jubilee. I guess you could say, "Go to the convent and see the world."

I hope and pray every day that God will send us more vocations. The superiors are stretching our personnel to get the work done, and we are having to hire some laypeople in areas like the kitchen and in our altar bread bakery. I also hope we preserve our way of life, the contemplative Benedictine way of life.

Father

ALBAN BOULTWOOD

Born 1911

Father Alban is a member of the Benedictine community at St. Anselm's Abbey in Washington, D.C.

❁

I come to Washington to install an exhibition of my paintings in the rotunda of the Cannon House Office Building on Capitol Hill. At the same time I am here to meet Father Alban, the former abbot and founding prior of St. Anselm's Abbey. When I arrive at the abbey, it is dinnertime and I am shown directly to the dining hall. The dining arrangements are different from any monastery I have visited before. Instead of the usual cafeteria-style serving, the dinner here is served course by course, like in a real restaurant. At the conclusion of dinner I am told that I will have to wait a bit to meet Father Alban, as he has been one of the food servers and needs to finish up in the kitchen. What a profound lesson in Benedictine humility! This deeply revered elder just served me my dinner.

Father Alban

When I entered the monastery in 1929, life was simpler, and society was more settled and stable. The church and monastic institutions were established and accepted. Contrast that with the confusion young people encounter today. It was much simpler for us.

At the age of eleven I was sent to a boarding school run by the Benedictines at Fort Augustus, in the Highlands of Scotland. There I came to know good men and to experience something of their way of life. I was attracted, applied to enter, and was accepted in 1929. At the age of eighteen there was surely not a profound understanding of the full scope of monastic life, but there was good will and the desire to learn. In this, as in many other things, it is only as life unfolds that we learn the true character of the vocation, as must happen, I think, in a good marriage.

My early years were, of course, in formation. There was first the novitiate year of exclusively spiritual and monastic study, after which I was sent to study philosophy for two years in Rome. This was followed by four years at Edinburgh University, in the field of English literature and language. After a further three years of the study of theology, I was ordained to the priesthood, ten years after entering the monastery. But then, in 1939, World War II broke out, and eight of us from the community volunteered as chaplains with the British Army. For the next six years I served in England, North Africa, Italy (including the Battle of Monte Cassino), and Austria.

I was discharged in 1946 and returned to the monastery in Scotland. I expected to live and work there for the rest of my life, but almost at once I was sent to the priory which

Fort Augustus was founding here in Washington, D.C., and I served as its superior for the next twenty-nine years. It was a very interesting time. St. Anselm's was growing, and it became an independent abbey in 1961.

Then came the Second Vatican Council, which led to a time of intense self-examination for communities. The ideals and documents of the Council were splendid, but we did not always apply them wisely. Mistakes were made, and tension was felt in the communities, which tended to divide into conservative and progressive elements. Superiors were often caught in the middle, and it was not an easy period for them. Yet it did lead to a stronger sense of community, of our responsibility for one another and for ourselves.

In 1975, I retired from the office of abbot. There is a wise custom that the former abbot should leave to give the new abbot a clear opportunity, so I went as chaplain to a group of Benedictine sisters in Virginia for six months. But soon after I returned to St. Anselm's another group of sisters asked me for help, because their chaplain had died suddenly. I said I would come for a month or so until they could find a permanent replacement, but in fact it lasted fifteen years. It proved to be a very pleasant period, after the responsibilities of the abbot's office. The sisters were running an academy on two hundred acres of lovely Virginia countryside, much enjoyed by my border collie and myself. During the years with the sisters I always had one day a week at St. Anselm's and all the summer vacation periods, and in 1990 I returned to the abbey permanently.

I should mention that I managed to do some writing during that period, and three books were published: *Alive to God, Into His Splendid Light,* and *Christ in Us.*

❁

In thinking of what has given me happiness in my life, sometimes one dares to think and hope that one has been used by the Lord in some way for the good of his people. Any priest and any religious superior may occasionally recognize that in spite of his own weakness and unworthiness, he seems to have been an instrument for some kind of good to others. In what has given me unhappiness, it is probably the reverse of the preceding. One feels one has been a disappointment to the Lord and to others. All we can do is to leave it to divine mercy. I have no regrets in having chosen the monastic life, but of course there have been disappointments, but these came from unreal hopes or human failures.

It is the breadth and depth of the Benedictine spirituality that attracts me. It is very basic. The monastic rule is an attempt to take the gospel and bring it down to the practical daily life of prayer, work, and community. Personally, I need the support of a regular routine and the support of the community. We are social beings, even in our religion, perhaps especially in our religion, and we do need one another. I have never really wanted the life of a solitary hermit. The common goals and common efforts strengthen us. Benedictine work is very flexible; we were not founded for a specific mission. We are about community and prayer, and any work that fits with that is acceptable. But the work should be of some service to people.

It is a very human sort of life. Perhaps some people may see our celibacy as inhuman, and perhaps it would be if it meant a renunciation of love rather than sexual activity. But celibacy is meant to be a very positive kind of life in which there is plenty of love, though not the exclusive, possessive love of the married life. It can be a very happy and fulfilling life. You may not have your own family home in the ordinary sense, yet you can be at home everywhere. Prayer, work, and community are all involved in the bodily aspect of each individual. We are not disembodied, and the physical is dealt with in the Rule in many ways.

I love the second to last chapter of the Rule that deals with "the good zeal." It is a beautiful summary of the whole Rule, dealing with charity, care, mutual respect, and mutual obedience.

The Rule is not superficial; it does not prescribe arbitrary pieties or mortifications. It is concerned with the gospel ideals of following Christ in simplicity and poverty, with a practical daily routine. It tries to establish a reality, not just talk of ideals. We indeed need ideals, but we cannot live on ideals. We need to live on the level of humble reality. Indeed the Rule anticipates all sorts of failures but encourages perseverance. G. K. Chesterton said, in typical paradox, "If a thing is worth doing, it's worth doing badly." When the ideals are so high, the call so insistent, then it's worth setting out on the way, even though we may fall short in attainment. I find both the spirit and the humanity of the Rule helpful and attractive. The vows we take all involve the main instincts or driving forces of our nature. The vow of poverty balances our instinct of possessiveness, celibacy balances our affections, obedience our pride and willfulness. The vows are not just restrictions. They are positive instruments to be used to direct these powerful driving forces in the direction of eternal values, rather than personal, selfish values. The paradox is that it is precisely in giving of oneself that one finds true fulfillment. Every good psychologist knows this, and the Lord Jesus expressed it strikingly in the words that one who seeks his own life loses it, while the one who is willing to lose his life will find it. The Rule helps us to give ourselves. We cannot really do much about sanctifying ourselves; what we can do is to give ourselves, and let the Lord do the sanctifying. At the end of the Rule, Benedict calls it "a little rule for beginners." That is very comforting, because we always feel, and rightly so, that we are just beginning.

A monastic community must first be a true family; then it will have something to offer to others, and can invite them in. To build up that family, as with any family, a certain privacy or seclusion is needed. Then, when there is a solid unity within, others can be invited to share it. People come as guests, to share in our prayer, and perhaps to seek spiritual direction. Further, many monasteries have oblates, men and women living in the world, pursuing their careers, but truly part of the monastic family. They follow the spirit of the Rule, share our liturgies, and support the community by their prayer and with material help if they can.

St. Benedict calls for special care of the aged and of the young, and he has whole chapters on food and drink, even on clothing. The supernatural must be based on the natural, community must be based on family. It is not a matter of emotional sentimental feeling or demonstration, but deep, true goodwill and caring, especially in time of need. There must be a genuine family spirit, but when you are living together all your life, a certain restraint is also necessary. There must be respect for the ultimate mystery of each person. This is one reason why the tradition of silence in monastic life is so important. There is a proper protection needed for the privacy and dignity of each individual.

We live by values, and one important value is surely faithfulness, genuine commitment. In our time, freedom is much misunderstood, and often is made an idol. But freedom is only half the human act. It is indeed freedom that makes an act human, but it is how that freedom is used that makes the act good or bad. The choice of an evil thing does not make it right, just because it was freely chosen. The moral value of our act lies in how our freedom is used. I think monks can give witness in our society that it is possible to live a stable community life with other human beings, in peace, loving service, and faithful lifelong commitment. That might be an important contribution. I am confident that the monastic vocation will endure. Our history has been through many ups and downs over fifteen hundred years. But it remains a good way of life for those who can follow it.

Sister

ANNELLA GARDNER

Born 1918

Sister Annella is a member of the Benedictine community at Sacred Heart Monastery in Richardton, North Dakota.

❁

The golden hills of western North Dakota seem an appropriately reclusive setting for a Benedictine monastery, but there are surprises in store for a visitor to Sacred Heart. The first surprise is evident from some distance. Two huge wind turbines rise into the sky. The turbines, installed to provide electricity for the monastic community, at times produce so much extra power that the sisters sell the excess back to the local power company. The second surprise is the monastery's herd of llamas. They are in well-kept corrals and pastures where the adult animals graze, while the young prance and play. This ranch is a commercial enterprise of the sisters, who raise the llamas as breeding stock, therapy animals, pets, and for wool production.

The elder chosen by the community for my meeting is Sister Annella. When I want to know her thoughts on the future, her quick reply, with a smile, is, "Don't worry about it." Later I come to understand that her advice was meant very seriously. Sister Annella is a woman who has undergone tremendous change in her life. She helped to build institution after institution, and many times circumstances dictated that she then hand them over to others and move on. She has learned that change is inevitable and that it is our place to adapt and grow.

Sister Annella

I KNEW no nuns growing up. I was raised in a small mission community called Sanish, on the Fort Berthold Reservation in North Dakota. Sanish is an Indian word meaning "good people." But that is not what our little town was known for, quite the opposite. It was known as a tough town with troubles one usually associates with big cities. My father was in law enforcement most of my growing years. The priest made it to our community about five times a year. My mother was church sacristan from the time the church started in 1915 until she died. Observing my mother was what gave me a religious background. We had very little formal religious instruction. I don't know where I got the idea, but very young I decided I wanted to be a nun. The wish grew with me all the way to my high school years. The only thing I knew about nuns were bits and pieces I read in Catholic magazines. There is a television advertisement for a car that features an eagle swooping down on a very calm lake and grabbing a fish out of the water. Whenever I see that ad, it reminds me of my vocation. I feel that God simply swooped down and grabbed me. Joining with so little knowledge, I had no idea of what this life would be like. I don't know what I expected — I just wanted to join. There was a sense of mystery that was good. It was a sense of awe. Young people joining today have little of that. I think there should be some surprises — some mystery.

In high school I knew I wanted to be a nun, but I had no idea of how to join and what to do. A priest finally brought me over to the Benedictines at Garrison, North Dakota, and that set me on my course. It really was like God and the eagle.

I've never considered anything else. In 1936, at the age of eighteen, I joined the Benedictines.

Frankly, other than the balance between work and prayer, I don't think there was much difference between the monastery and my home. I came from a strict home to a strict convent. It was just more of the same. At the convent, prayer became more important in my life. I have always loved the Divine Office. We were given the time for meditation but never given any training, but it became an important time of the day for me.

I was sent to school for two years and received a two-year teaching certificate. I then spent a year in the novitiate and then was sent out teaching. I spent my first year teaching primarily the eighth grade in Karlsruhe, North Dakota. Then, in 1942, I made final vows and I was sent to St. Catherine's College in St. Paul, Minnesota, to get a degree in science teaching as we were taking over a high school and a science teacher was needed. When I first came to the monastery I told them I wanted to be a nurse. They said I needed to be a teacher. They were right, and I have never regretted a day of my teaching. I loved teaching biology and science. I feel God was guiding the superior when she decided I was to be a teacher. I taught for forty years, until 1983.

I taught at St. Leo's in Minot, North Dakota, for fifteen years. We had taken over the school from the Franciscans at the request of the bishop, and it had caused the Franciscans sorrow in the process. Then, after fifteen years, the bishop decided that the school should be handed over to the Ursulines, as they could fill more teaching positions than we could. It was the bishop's decision, but we pretended as if it had been our decision to avoid the same problems that occurred when we took over the school from the Franciscans. It created a great deal of sadness for us. The sorrow was really in the way it was all handled.

I was then principal of Sacred Heart Academy in Minot. I also was studying for a master's in administration and received the degree in 1960 from St. Thomas College in St. Paul.

In 1962, I was sent to Bogotá, Colombia, to start a girls' school there. It was to be an English-speaking school. We started with sixty-three girls, grades one to four. We spoke no Spanish and they spoke no English. The parents did not want us to speak Spanish. We did hire some local teachers to help in the process, and we had an English-speaking teacher and a Spanish-speaking teacher for the same grade. Each year we would add a grade until we had all twelve. We added two sections of girls, seventy in all, each year. We bought land and built our own school, adding two rooms each year as we grew. We ended up with forty classrooms and nearly eight hundred students. It was a struggle, but I wouldn't trade those thirteen years for anything. It was such a challenge. We stayed independent of the diocese. They helped at first, but we then went off on our own. We had been asked to go down there and start a school, and we did. It was God's will, and we would do it, and we did do it. Looking back on it, I think the people in Colombia taught us as much as we taught them. We quickly learned that even though we were Americans who thought we knew it all, we didn't know it all. We learned a great deal from them. They were a people very strong on courtesy, gratitude, and loyalty.

In 1975, we dwindled down to three sisters left in Bogotá. The monastery back in America voted to close the school. We then gave the school to the diocese. I had already begun to feel that our time was over there before the decision was made. I had taken a retreat in New Mexico, and I had a vision of sorts that led me to Psalm 32. When I went to the Psalm the entire page appeared blank except for the verse:

I will instruct you and teach you the way you should go;
I will give you counsel with my eye upon you.

I didn't know the answer as such, but I was sure that God was guiding me. It was hard to give up the school, but I felt God was with us. I went to the bishop in Bogotá and said, "Here is our school, you may have it." They have continued the school as an English-speaking all girls' school to this day.

I loved teaching. I was always free to teach as I thought I needed to. Outside of my religious life, teaching was my greatest joy. In my teaching I enjoyed explaining things. I did not mind answering questions — as many as were needed to find understanding. Many of my students went on to jobs in the science fields and have kindly given me credit for helping them on their way. It was a great inspiration to keep teaching as well as I could. Even now, after being gone from Bogotá for over twenty-five years, my students have invited me back to Colombia to thank me for the school and their education. It is such a wonderful feeling of gratitude. I'm very much looking forward to the trip to see how the school has developed over the years. I feel Benedictines should start things and move on.

In 1975, we came home from Colombia. I took a one-year sabbatical at the monastery. It was then that I had to confront the changes of Vatican II that had been taking place in America for the thirteen years of our absence. They hadn't really affected us much in Bogotá. I like to take my time in making decisions; I don't like jumping from one thing to another. So I eventually did make the change to the short habit, but I have never had any desire to go into the colors of street clothing. For one thing I did not want to get up every morning and have to decide what I was going to wear. With the short habit, I know exactly what I will wear each morning. When I came home from Bogotá, I was at the point where I could accept what others were doing, but I was not going to do it myself until I understood and decided if I would be comfortable with the changes. Much of the turmoil had passed by the time I came home. I also decided to keep the veil. I am more comfortable with people knowing that I am a sister. It is what I wanted when I entered in 1936, and it is what I am comfortable with almost seventy years later.

I then went to Ryan High School back in Minot. I did secretarial and receptionist work for them for seven years. I did some teaching, but I was shocked by the attitude of the students; it had changed drastically in my time out of the country. There was such a lack of respect. It seemed a waste of my time trying to handle an unruly classroom. After my years there I went to Bismarck, North Dakota, as the assistant administrator at St. Vincent's Nursing Home. I said I would go there for three years and I stayed nine. In 1992, I came back to the monastery, where I now help with the scheduling of spirituality groups and also with the monastery reception duties.

I have spent most of my life in the teaching field. There I did what was needed. Everything was on the hour. The bell rang to wake us in the morning and the lights went out to put us to bed at night. Meals, prayer, everything needed to be done on time. Punctuality was important. We had special times for recreation, usually after lunch and dinner.

I have always been given the very best of physical care. In 1949, I spent two months in bed, another time I spent eighteen months in bed, and more recently I was down for two months. A person can expect to be well taken care of physically as a Benedictine.

In the early years we were given was what called "professional courtesy" by the doctors. They did not charge us when we needed their services. And for years the Franciscan hospital we used did not charge us either. We also had free passes to travel on the trains. Because we were in the religious life, there was an understanding in the society that we were poor people and dedicated to helping others and, as such, people helped us.

There is also a physical stability to this life. This is my home. There is a stability to both past and present members of this community. There are now only four people alive who were professed when I made my vows. All the rest are younger. But this is my home. I made my vow of stability to this group. The community changes but the commitment remains. The new people fall in as part of us so quickly, you soon can't imagine the community without them. But you don't come for the people. You come because it's the life you want and need to live.

In the Rule of St. Benedict the chapter on the procurator, the monk who decides on the allocation of goods, struck me very forcefully. I agree with the need to be accommodating to people's needs, and I also agree in not going too far. The Rule shows us that there are real needs and necessities, but they are not to be confused with wants.

The last chapter of the Rule on the good zeal of the monks has also been a favorite of mine. Plus, the Rule's stress on obedience has been special to me; having wanted to be a nurse and then being requested to become a teacher, I was obedient. And in being so I feel I was following the grace of God as shown through my superiors.

I believe honesty and integrity are very important values to uphold and promote. We need to face the consequences of our actions. I think back to my father and that he had only a fifth-grade education, but to him a handshake was as important as a written contract. My father was not a perfect saint, but he was a good man. He upheld the law, and he had honesty and integrity. So many of our government officials today seem to be lacking in morals that are perceptible. I wonder if it all doesn't go back to the "me, myself, and I" philosophy that has been developing throughout the twentieth century. Nothing is wrong unless you get caught. We need good examples of moral people. I had teachers who were good, honest people, and they modeled morals for me. They talk today of posting the Ten Commandments in schools; that certainly won't teach young people morals. Hillary Rodham Clinton has often used the old African proverb, "It takes a village to raise a child." I believe that, and we had that in the rather tough little community that I grew up in. If anything happened in the town, people were there to help. There was no question of who was a Baptist or Catholic or Methodist. My dad used to put up ice in the winter as there was no refrigeration in those days. If anyone in the community got sick and needed ice, my father would not sell it to them—he insisted that the ice be given to them free of charge, even though it was an important part of our livelihood. People took a real interest in one another.

Where are today's children going to learn morals and values? So many families are broken or busy, and few people even know their neighbors. There are many good people out there to learn from, but we so seldom hear about them. The news seems obsessed with the bad and the sensational.

Still, I do have hopes for the future. I hope we will gain new vocations. Our membership will be dropping off rapidly. We have about twenty-five in the house now, and half of us are above eighty years old, and we have few that are younger than fifty. It's hard to say what will happen to the community if we don't get new members. I do feel that somehow we are going to go on. Our community has been in existence for over eighty years. We are a small group, but I feel we are a great group. I don't think God will let that dwindle out. The community will undoubtedly change. People coming into the community now have a completely different background than we did in the 1930s. Each new member puts a different flavor into the community. All these new flavors are going to create a new community flavor. I don't know if it will be chocolate or strawberry, but it will be different from what we have today. If I had to do it again, coming in and knowing nothing of monastic life (now I think I know it all), I would do it again.

Father

EUGENE W. DEHNER

1914–2004

Father Eugene was a member of the Benedictine community at St. Benedict's Abbey in Atchison, Kansas.

St. Benedict's Abbey was founded in 1857, making it one of the country's oldest monasteries. Today it is dominated by a massive abbey church designed by Barry Byrne, a student of Frank Lloyd Wright. The imposing structure, with its 125-foot tower and seating capacity of 650, was completed in 1957 to mark the centennial of the abbey. On the hillside below the abbey lies Benedictine College, where Father Eugene had been teaching most of his life. I felt very comfortable talking with Father Eugene, as he was an academic through and through, and so it was much like chatting with one of my colleagues at the university where I teach.

Father Eugene

LIKE MANY young Catholic boys of my time, I had some thought of becoming a religious of some kind when I was only twelve or thirteen. In my senior year of high school one of the sisters asked me if I had ever considered becoming a priest. That surprised me and got me thinking even more about the possibility. The Benedictines from Atchison were taking care of my home parish in Burlington, Iowa. In those years seniors in high school didn't have the huge amount of literature on which college to choose as they do now. My father suggested that I go to Atchison and study at Benedictine College. I had made up my mind to study for the priesthood and possibly to join the Benedictines. I liked the idea of each Benedictine monastery being autonomous.

As a college freshman I started studying biology, and it became my major. After two years of college, I was allowed to enter the novitiate. I took my first vows in 1935. In 1937, I graduated from college with my biology degree and began my theology studies. I was ordained in 1940 and finished my theology studies in 1941. I then went directly to graduate school. There were some monks here at the abbey who opposed young monks going to graduate school. They said it changed the monk too much, while others said it was supposed to. I was fortunate in that they sent me to Cornell University for graduate work in biology, because most of the Catholic universities at that time didn't have strong Ph.D. programs in zoology. It was a rather last-minute decision. Classes started on a Monday, and on the Friday before I was told I could go. It was a hectic beginning, but providentially it all worked out. As it turned out, I was asked to offer a daily

Mass at the student religious center on campus and this has been going on ever since. I had very good professors and did my master's degree research on doves and my Ph.D. research on ducks.

My family has had a strong inclination toward the religious life. One of my brothers also became a Benedictine here at Atchison. Another brother became a Trappist in Georgia, one brother was temporarily a Trappist in New Mexico, one of my sisters became a Carmelite sister in San Diego, and, after my mother died in 1947, my father became a Trappist monk in Georgia as well. My dad had a wonderful sense of humor and spent the rest of his life, thirty more years, praying and raising chickens at the Trappist monastery.

I have worn three hats: the cowl of a monk, the biretta of a priest, and the mortarboard of a professor. Since I completed graduate school, most of my time has been taken up by my work as a professor. I remember my first day of teaching here at Benedictine College. I thought I was well prepared; I had my notes and materials all ready, but I ended up running out of "stuff." There were ten full minutes remaining in the class, and I could not think of another thing to say. After that first time, though, I always had more than enough to say. I was first assigned to a residence hall and lived on campus, supervising the students and teaching my classes. But during most of my college career, I lived in the monastery and during the school year regularly went out on weekends with parish work in the area. I was in Topeka, Kansas, and other cities but spent most of my time in St. Joseph, Missouri. That could be a bit tiring in that you would be gone all weekend and then have to get ready for Monday classes.

As a monk living in the abbey, I was also keeping up the prayer schedule. Until the mid-fifties we were getting up at

4:00 a.m. for Matins and Lauds, which lasted about an hour and a quarter. Besides a "community" Mass there were three shorter sessions of the Divine Office during the day.

Some of the other things I have done were to work at a boys' summer camp in the late 1930s and 1940s. I also spent two summers as a chaplain in Yellowstone National Park. I had a long association with the National Federation of Catholic College Students, and, after having been a regional moderator for five years, was national chaplain from 1962 to 1965.

One of the objectives in my teaching career was to help prepare students for graduate and professional school. Conservatively speaking, we had about three hundred students go on to medical or dental school during my time. Most were biology majors. I put the emphasis on lab work and experiential learning. I think it was the right way to prepare students. I believe we should think of teaching and study as work, an especially dignified kind of work, dealing with the souls and minds of people. This is correctly known as a profession. I'm very happy with having spent my life as a college professor. I don't regret a minute of it. Thanks to the goodness of God, I think I have received many blessings in return for any sacrifices and efforts I have made on behalf of students. I taught for thirty-eight years and retired at the age of seventy. I was having considerable trouble with osteoarthritis in my knees at that time, and so I was ready to take a rest.

The most joy in my life has come from success over a long period of time as a teacher as shown in feedback from students. I have always liked working with my hands, and I thoroughly enjoyed some of the complex lab work we did. It created a deep feeling of accomplishment.

There has also been some sorrow in my life. One of those was the sadness I felt when a relatively large number of monks quit the abbey in what I call the revolution of the sixties. They went back on their vows, especially that of stability. One of those to leave was my own brother, and this gave me some sorrow.

I certainly have no regrets in having chosen a monastic life. I thank God every day I wound up this way. People seem to be very timid now about making choices, especially life-forming choices such as marriage or joining a religious order. People seem to have a hard time making firm long-term commitments. I prayed like the dickens before I made vows. I've had many critical times, like in marriage where you get to the point where you might betray one another, and the same thing can happen to a priest or monk. I've been fortunate to make the right choices in serious situations, for which I thank God. Maybe it has been someone's prayers that have helped me.

I'm very grateful to God and to my religious community of St. Benedict's Abbey for untold blessings and unfailing support through all my years as a Benedictine. The deliberately made vows of obedience, stability, and conversion of life have liberated me to give fully of my best efforts and energy on behalf of the wider family of the church and state. I do not know, or particularly care, what other people think, but I can say that I cannot imagine things having worked out better for me.

I have always appreciated the Benedictine vow of stability. I always knew where my home base was. If I wasn't off on some kind of business, I knew I would be here and that someday I would be buried here.

Life at the abbey requires a great deal of physical movement. The abbey building itself is very large, and a considerable amount of walking is needed to get around. When teaching, there was a nice walk to the campus and back, usually several times a day. Just the necessary walking has been good physical exercise. We are always well taken care of physically; medical and dental needs are always seen to.

St. Benedict calls the Divine Office, our community prayer, "the work of God." This system of prayer provides the daily spiritual food for the monastic. This has been one of the things that I have enjoyed about the Benedictine life. You have the Psalms ready-made for prayer. You don't have to worry about generating your own prayer. The Divine Office is a great part of your prayer life.

I found insight in Benedict's instruction that we should see the person of Christ in the abbot, that we should receive guests as if we are receiving Christ, and that we should see the person of Christ in the sick for whom we are caring. I have many favorite chapters in the Rule of St. Benedict: Chapters 1 through 7, especially the parts on obedience and humility; Chapters 31 through 41, the care of the tools and goods of the community; Chapter 72 on the good zeal of monks; and Chapter 73, encouraging us to go on to greater knowledge and virtue.

The monastic life teaches you to be very tolerant. You have to learn to accept the characteristics and foibles of others, or you simply don't last as a monk. I found the same thing with students. I tried to treat each student as an individual, and I think they appreciated that. I feel I am receptive to the differences in people and different cultures. I always tried to treat everyone equally.

When I think of values, three words come to my mind: study, prayer, and meditation. These are key monastic values we have. Study is the first to me, in that you need to study and deepen your understanding, and this is then utilized and reflected in your prayer and meditation. I feel education can be a real asset to your spiritual life. Prayer is an essential communication with God. The beauty of the monastic life is the communal prayer. We all pray together. If at all possible we all come to choir for the prayer known as the Divine Office. Private prayer is also important, and I spend time each day in private prayer as well as our group prayer.

Thinking of values for general society, I would say honesty and a sense of responsibility are very important. Both of these relate to a sense of unselfishness.

In my teaching I did not talk a great deal about religion, but some of my students in retrospect have said they remember in my teaching a love of science as God's creation. I'm glad they got that. I do remember beginning each class with a prayer that God would activate our cerebral hemispheres and modulate our medulla oblongata. I am in agreement with the diplomat and historian George Kennan, who once said that in professions such as teaching and the priesthood one should not anxiously inquire into the results of one's efforts; "The effort itself is its own reward and the results are the concern of a Higher Authority."

I have hopes for the future. I hope some members of our community will stay with academic work. Some of our younger people now seem interested in it. I am optimistic about the future. I've learned to be so over the years. When I came here the monastery was in debt over a million dollars.

You can imagine what that looked like in 1930. Some people wanted to fold up the place and disband, while others wanted to stick with it. I've always followed the policy of sticking with it. I think there will always be a St. Benedict's Abbey. I hope that in thirty or forty years it will be even better than what we have now.

Sister

MARY GREGORY CUSHING

Born 1913

Sister Mary Gregory is a member of the Benedictine Sisters of Perpetual Adoration in Tucson, Arizona.

Tucson is a long way from South Dakota, both in distance and culture. Coming from the snow and gray of a Midwestern spring, Sammy and I enjoy our drive through the Southwest with its brilliant light and warm colors. The Benedictine monastery in Tucson is beautiful, with ochres, blues, and pinks of the Southwest covering the graceful curving lines of the architecture. Inside, the chapel is breathtaking. Elegant simplicity and richness of materials create a sacred space worthy of the sisters' worship. Yet the beauty of the monastery's exterior and interior pales next to the beauty of the sisters' choir. Their singing and chanting is truly angelic. During the 1980s, this peaceful place with its gentle inhabitants harbored refugees escaping the horrific wars in Central America. Offering refuge was a bold expression of the Benedictine tradition of compassion and hospitality. Sister Mary Gregory represents all of these qualities very well.

Sister Mary Gregory

I GRADUATED from high school in 1932 and worked for four years. When I finally determined to follow the call to religious life, I wanted to be a missionary "to save souls." After a brief talk with the mother general of a missionary order, I decided daily hard work and childcare in the bush were not for me.

After reading that St. Teresa of Avila "saved more souls by her life of prayer, than did St. Francis Xavier in all his mission work," I decided to pursue a life of prayer. That's why I first went to the Carmelites. I loved it. I was there for life, or so I thought. But a problem came at Lent when they prepared for their great fast. The sisters felt I was too frail for the fast and penance, and I was asked to leave. My saddest day was the day I was sent away from the Carmelites. My ego took a beating that day. Another great sorrow had happened immediately before going to the Carmelites. I was staying with a friend, resting before entering the monastery, when the house burnt to the ground. I barely escaped with my life, but my dear friend was burned to death. She was a beautiful person.

A Carmelite sister asked me if I had heard of the Benedictine sisters in Clyde, Missouri. Of course I hadn't. But I wrote, was accepted, and now, here I am. I was twenty-five years old when I joined in 1938. The day I was accepted for perpetual vows was a great, great joy!

In the novitiate, I started learning to play organ. Wherever there was a need for an organist through the years, I fulfilled the charge until I retired from playing in 1992.

I've been called to work in the correspondence departments in many of our monasteries: Kansas City, Mundelein in Illinois, San Diego (these three have since been closed), and

Tucson. Two other primary duties have been sewing for the community and working in the altar bread departments of the monasteries. My duties here in Tucson at the present time are as archivist and chronicler and part-time receptionist. It has been a wonderful life.

I feel hospitality is very important. St. Benedict said that in receiving guests, we welcome Christ himself. I believe that the Spirit of God is in all people, whether they know it or not.

I have always loved the world. I wanted to save the world, to bring all to Christ. But through years of prayer and study, I have come to learn that everyone will attain the glory God has ordained for them if they will turn to him in prayer. I only need to deepen my own spiritual life through observance of the precepts of the gospel, embodied in the Rule of Benedict.

St. Benedict asks us to seek God, to seek him in community. There are some parts of the Rule of Benedict that are not possible to fulfill today. But through our constitutions and policies and the direction and leadership of the prioress, the tradition lives on. The Benedictine tradition of *lectio* is coming to the forefront in our times. I have been practicing this for some years and have shared my practice with many. *Lectio* is the prayerful reading of Scripture, meditating on the message, and asking how it can be applied to my own life at this time. Then one sits in silence before the Lord, resting in him, to be nourished by the Word and receive direction from him. I love the last chapter of the Rule where Benedict promises that if I keep this "least of all Rules which has been written for beginners," I will surely "attain the lofty heights of wisdom and virtue. . . ."

The Benedictine way of life is a stable life of balance between work and prayer. It is the giving of prime time to God and our spiritual life. When not worshipping God with the community or in private, I am doing his work. It is a life lived in God for others — for the world. The community life is one of sharing joys and sorrows and supporting one another. The Rule of Benedict is strong in urging us to bear with one another, to forgive one another if there is that need, and to be kind and humble. St. Benedict's teaching on humility is very important to me. Such a community is a great gift of God. It is a wonderful feeling to know you are part and parcel of that kind of love in community. The most important values to uphold are community life, silence, and the acceptance of others as they are. We can promote these by sharing with our brothers and sisters any part of our Benedictine life that is possible for us. We can invite them to experience the silence and solitude of our lives by making retreats here. We can share the importance of the acceptance of others as they are, whenever people come to us for help in their spiritual life.

I have great hopes because I trust in the guidance of the Holy Spirit. I hope that people will follow their good inspirations under the leadership of this Holy Spirit. I certainly hope for more vocations to the religious life, especially in our community. We have much to share in a world fragmented by divorce, drugs, and the many other problems of modern life. If families could learn from Benedictines the joy and peace of family, living and praying together, the world would be a different place altogether.

Father

BERTHOLD RICKER

1907–2002

Father Berthold was a member of the Benedictine community at St. John's Abbey in Collegeville, Minnesota.

❁

St. John's is a most impressive monastery with its distinctive abbey church designed by Marcel Breuer, its well-known university, and its lovely surroundings of lakes, ponds, and woods. Its large population of monks makes it a somewhat less personal place to visit than some smaller monasteries, but the hospitality is just as heartfelt.

Whenever I mentioned to locals that I had come to meet the former prior, Berthold Ricker, their eyes softened and they smiled. I went to see Father Berthold in the monastery's infirmary, where he was living because of his frail health. His voice was halting but full of gentleness and sincerity. We took frequent breaks and sat on the porch and enjoyed the beauty of the Minnesota woods surrounding us. Some weeks later as I was working in my studio, I received a telephone call. The voice at the other end was barely discernable. It was Father Berthold. He asked me if there was anything he could do to help me with my book. I was very touched and understood even more the softened eyes and smiles.

Father Berthold

GROWING UP in Freeport, Minnesota, we had a Benedictine pastor, Father Meinrad. He was a little short fellow but real dynamite. He was full of energy and very genuine. He used to say that he might occasionally blow up like a teapot but would always cool down rapidly.

My Aunt Mary also influenced my interest in Benedictine life. She was my mother's sister, and she became the woman in our family after my mother was hospitalized. I owed much to her prayers and the personal sacrifice in her life to be with us. She never left us while I was growing up. She died at the age of ninety-eight at St. Benedict Center in St. Cloud, Minnesota, while I was chaplain there.

I was the only child in the family, and my mother was institutionalized when I was eight years old with what was then called falling sickness and is now known as epilepsy. In those days they had nothing to treat it. I was a bit lonely as a child, and the Benedictines seemed a very large family. I could have all kinds of brothers there.

I attended St. John's High School here at Collegeville beginning in 1918. In my third year at the high school, I received my vocation; I became aware that I wanted to join the order.

I graduated from high school in 1923. I joined the novitiate at St. John's in 1925, took first vows in 1926. I was studying and teaching at the same time and keeping pretty busy. I began studying for the priesthood and was ordained in 1931.

After my ordination I spent five years as assistant to priests in several parishes. After the teaching I had been doing at St. John's, the parish work seemed very difficult. Preparing and giving sermons on Sunday was a real job for me. I was never very good at public speaking. I have always been more of a one-to-one person. But after my first year was about three-quarters over, I began to see what parish life was really like. I thought of all the services we were providing for the people — marriages, baptisms, confirmations, comfort in sickness, funerals, and many others — I could see that it was very important work, work in which you could help people.

I was then assigned as chaplain to the men's reformatory in St. Cloud, where I stayed for twelve years. Once I got into my work at the reformatory I really enjoyed it. It was mostly a one-to-one situation. It took a while to learn the ropes of how to get things done, but I received good advice. I was told to always get permission from those in control and to never try to bluff the inmates, always be honest with them. It was excellent advice. I had some successes and some agonizing experiences as well. I remember one fellow who came to see me; he was connected to a murder. We had a good talk, and as he was about to leave, I got up to walk out with him. I shook his hand and patted him on the back, and to my surprise he broke down crying. He said, "Father, you are the first person to pat me on the back since my mother, who used to do it when I left for school." I thought to myself how hungry that man was for something positive instead of the constant negativity that surrounded him.

In 1949, I was sent to Mexico as prior of a new foundation. We staffed a boys' school there that grew from five hundred students to eventually three thousand. In 1956, I was assigned to begin a new boys' school, also in Mexico.

In 1958, I returned to St. Cloud as assistant at St. Augustine's Church and became pastor there in 1960 for four years. In 1964, I became prior here at St. John's and remained in the position for eleven years. That's quite a few years as prior. Much of the job was helping people in many different ways. I tried to make it a policy that if the monks had any complaining to do, they were to come to me first and not bother the abbot. I didn't mind them letting their anxieties out when they needed to, and we could discuss and argue about it. Sometimes, if it was important enough, we then needed to go to the abbot. I tried to do my job with kindness and understanding. If someone came to me and asked for a Greek dictionary, I had to base my decision on their needs and not my needs. Just because I wasn't in need of one didn't mean he wasn't. It was that way for many things. You can't use yourself as a model for the needs of others.

Then from 1975 until 1993 I was a chaplain at nursing homes, first at Assumption Nursing Home in Cold Spring, Minnesota, and then at St. Benedict's Center in St. Cloud. I enjoyed working with the seniors; after all, I was one too. I had a great empathy for them from my experiences with my family, first having my mother hospitalized when I was so young, and second with my granddad who lived to be over ninety-nine years old. He was with us for a long time. I understood his problems and difficulties in growing old. In the hard times of the mid-1930s, he used to go out and give candy to the neighborhood children. I found working with the elderly very rewarding. Then in the early 1990s, heart problems and broken hips ended my days as chaplain. Now I live on a floor of the monastery with about twenty-five other monks who have health problems and need care. These men have a variety of ailments and some are very serious, but the grace with which they accept and live with their problems is amazing. I admire them; they make the best of it. Everyone is an example for everyone else. I am so well taken care of. I have been a priest and a monk for over seventy years. I have always known where I belonged, and I have always felt the support of my community whether in Mexico or here at St. John's.

The greatest joy in my life has been to have the faith and have it strengthen over the years. The goodness of the Lord and his mercy have given me great joy. Being a priest has also given me a great deal of joy. I have to agree with one of my fellow monks here who used to love to hear confessions. That may sound a bit strange, but he said that hearing so many good people who want to be even better restored his confidence in humanity. I see that as a good way of looking at it. It is such a privilege to be a bridge between people and the Lord. He is everything. Any richness in us is because of him.

With all the joys of my life, I do have some regrets. I feel I have not lived up to everything I wanted to. I feel I could have worked harder when I was in the parish, visiting more people. It is easy to get caught up in the administrative aspect of parish life. It can be hard to get around to eight hundred families. I always prepared for my preaching, but I feel it could have been better. I was not the pastor I would have liked to have been.

Benedictine life simplifies spirituality. Humility is a major highlight. Humility doesn't mean standing in a corner. It means an honest acknowledgment that who you are and what you are is a gift of God—completely.

We have an active prayer life with morning, noon, and evening prayer. We also have daily Mass at 5:00 p.m. I feel the Eucharist is a deeply important part of our spiritual life.

Benedictine life is family life. The Benedictine Rule is humanizing. The Benedictine life is a very human life. There is a strictness, but with moderation. You have the vow of poverty—you don't own things. You have the vow of chastity—you don't marry. You have the vow of obedience—you obey the abbot at the monastery and the bishop if you are working in a parish.

The Rule is very practical. It says that if you are working in the kitchen you should have enough help. It says that your clothes and shoes should fit you. It says you should get enough to eat. It says many things to lead you to a life of physical moderation.

The rank in the monastery is according to the date you entered the monastery, not age, education, ordination, or any other factor. You don't fight for position. You have your place. It creates good order. This order is enhanced by our autonomy as a monastery. We are not told what to do by some regional, national, or international authority. Our abbot is the authority as he is guided by the community. If you read the Rule of Benedict, which was written in the sixth century, you have to marvel at the psychological astuteness of the document. The Rule has been my guide. The Rule can keep you glued to what you need to be doing. I do especially like the Prologue. The first words—*Obsculta, o fili*—"Listen, my child!" That's the important thing. Listen!

The Rule's guidance that nothing should interfere with your love of Christ is a deep reminder to me of what I am to be doing. Honesty is an important value. We need to always be open with one another. If something is broken it needs to be reported to the appropriate person. Not so that punishment can be given but so that replacement can take place if necessary. It's just a matter of honesty. Another aspect of honesty is to be satisfied with who you are and make the most of it.

Loving your neighbor is a primary value of Benedictine life. How we can help and serve one another should be constantly on our minds. To be a Benedictine you need a thin skin in regard to yourself and a thick skin in regard to others. The conditioning of the monastic life makes you more aware of the excesses of the outside world. In the past thirty years, the influence of the church has diminished greatly in the outside world.

The Holy Spirit is guiding the church. It is in his hands. I see two options. First, the Holy Spirit may spread around enough vocations and our membership will stabilize. Second, he may let them dwindle to engage the laypeople more. It used to be that the monastics did everything. Now with the shortage of priests and sisters, the parishioners themselves are becoming more involved in the workings of the church.

We saw turmoil during the 1960s with about fifty to sixty monks leaving the monastery for lay life. But it was a time when every major institution in our culture was in turmoil—education, law, government, the military. The wise thing was that the Holy Spirit stepped in. With the wisdom of Pope John XXIII instituting Vatican II, the Catholic Church was the one major institution that put itself under the microscope and made large changes. We haven't seen the last of Vatican II; it still has much potential. I have every hope for the future of the church.

Sister

PLACIDIA HAEHN

1909–2002

Sister Placidia was a member of the Benedictine community at St. Placid Priory in Lacey, Washington.

❁

Nestled in the pines of western Washington, St. Placid Priory's contemporary architecture blends well into its rain-soaked surroundings. Sister Placidia, a venerated ex-prioress, was brought back to the priory for our meeting from a nearby convent where she lived in retirement. She was frail looking when I first met her, but with the frailty came a remarkable sense of grace, dignity, and — in a most tranquil way — authority. As her story unfolded, I learned that this wonderful woman had whole-heartedly devoted eighty years to her community, her students, and to God. In one part of our conversation regarding her teaching, her mind seemed to slip into the past and with a small smile she said, "I didn't raise my voice in class. Instead, if necessary, I would take a student's arm and squeeze it a bit. I did this because I remembered my calm, gentle mother doing this to me. She has been my inspiration and helped me all the way." As a fellow teacher I found this approach deeply moving. There were times when I used to do quite a bit of good-natured yelling to try to make points. But now, when I feel one of my art students needs some special support or encouragement, I will sometimes put my hand on his or her arm or shoulder and give a small, gentle squeeze. And each time it brings back the memory of Sister Placidia and her lesson of the caring squeeze.

Sister Placidia

WHEN IT COMES to why I joined the Benedictines, I must say I was too young to be aware of my decision. It has been said that the wind blows where it wishes, and that was the case with me. My father died when I was three and my mother died when I was twelve, and I was raised by my grandparents in central Minnesota. I have not had much sorrow in my life, except losing my parents at an early age was a deep sorrow. I'm sure I would have gained much from them had I been able to be with them longer.

I had a cousin who belonged to the community of St. Benedict's in St. Joseph, Minnesota. She would come and stay with my grandparents during her vacation. At the time I graduated from the eighth grade, we had no high school where I lived. My cousin said to me, "Did you ever think of becoming a sister?" I said that I had thought about it, and that she seemed happy there and I wondered if I might be happy there as well. She invited me to return with her after her vacation. I thought about it and discussed it with my grandparents. They said that if it was what I wanted it was fine with them. Before we went my cousin advised me to have my long curly hair cut so it wouldn't be so much work to keep up at the convent. It was hard, but I had it cut, and I was glad that I did. She was right. There was not time for fancy hair. I was fourteen or fifteen years old at that time. One of the reasons I decided to go was that they had a high school at St. Benedict's. My cousin said I could attend the high school, and if I thought the convent was not for me, I would not have to enter. I went back with her and it was wonderful. I enjoyed it. I finished my high school and did join. I was a postulant during high school, which helped me. During my senior year, I was sent to a school in Minneapolis to teach the kindergarten. It was a huge class that we had to divide. I knew nothing about teaching, but I was helped by a wonderful first-grade teacher, and I seemed to get by. They liked what I did anyway.

I joined in the mid-1920s and was sent out here to Washington in 1930. I thought I was going to the end of the world. I had never been out of Minnesota. We sat up on the train for two nights. There were about twelve sisters at Holy Rosary Convent in Tacoma, Washington, at that time. I remember going into the community room at the convent and looking around and thinking that if I made it for a year I'd be lucky. I was assigned to teach the third grade. I still knew very little about teaching, but with the grace of God and the help of the Holy Spirit it worked out, and I grew to enjoy it. I ended up staying twenty-three years in Tacoma. As we were teaching we took college courses and summer school for Washington State teaching and principal certification. It was a heavy load. Eventually I received my college degree. I taught many of the grades at Holy Rosary and was also principal for ten years. They were some of the happiest years of my life in spite of everything: all the hard work, the war, and the great poverty. The happiness was in doing what the Lord wanted us to do and being with each other. The foundation that we received in becoming Benedictines continues with us in our teaching. We are willing to extend ourselves to our students. We know this from how many of our students return to us years later and tell us what we meant to them. Not to be proud, but it happens often. Every Friday evening we would all get together for a social in the music room. We would bring our needlework or mending, and the highlight was that we took turns bringing a treat, usually something baked. For that part of the evening even our superior would leave her work and come down and join us. Those were wonderful evenings. We even started a little orchestra. We would make so many mistakes and then laugh and start all over again.

Due to the large number of sisters at the Benedictine community at St. Joseph, Minnesota, and their desire to come under pontifical jurisdiction and not diocesan, the Holy See requested the community divide into smaller groups. This was done, and we were designated as one. It began temporarily at the Holy Rosary Convent, and we began searching for a location. After a great deal of looking, we settled on a place at Mud Bay near Olympia. It was a wonderful place with a creek running by. Every year, the creek filled with salmon during the spawning period. We didn't realize the salmon were spawning, and two of the sisters went down to the creek and decided to supplement our table. One of the sisters had a garden rake that she would pull the salmon out with and bonk them on the head. They came back with a basket full. The next day they went back for more and noticed a couple of men watching them from the riverbank. Our sisters went on about their business. The men were game wardens. They came down and explained that the spawning salmon did not belong to us. The sisters were frightened; we were all frightened. But the wardens were good people and good friends with the priests at St. Martin's Abbey in Lacey. They later said they could find nothing in their regulations against taking salmon with a garden rake. That story was widely shared by the priests at St. Martin's.

I was elected first prioress, and our priory was called St. Placid. Later St. Martin's gave us this beautiful property across the highway from St. Martin's to build a new priory and school. It was a huge undertaking with all the fund-raising involved. We had such good laypeople helping us. Dr. Thomas Taylor, a dentist, headed the fund drive and did a wonderful job. We moved in 1961 and classes began. The priory has had such consistent help from two groups of laypeople, the Benedictine Boosters from Olympia and the St. Placid Club from Tacoma. It was a fine high school but closed twenty-four years later when so many Catholic schools were discontinued. I was reelected prioress once and then took a break and was elected again, making a total of twenty years. In 1978, I went to All Saints Convent in Puyallup, Washington, at first to "retire." But soon I became the librarian at the school and have been there ever since. There have been many problems and worries along the way, a lot of this and a lot of that, but somehow the Spirit has always been there and it has been a peaceful experience. I have always had the support of the community whenever I have needed it. Even in the difficult times of beginning the priory, I always had the community, God, the Blessed Mother, and many good laypeople to help me. Some laypeople have really been an encouragement to me. I was very young when I came, but I felt so at home. Everyone was so helpful and supportive, and here I am, some eighty years later. My greatest joy has been living in community. It is feeling secure, wanted, and being of service to others. Professionally, I have had joy in being available and being as much help as possible. I have had much joy in the many friends I have been blessed with.

I had faith as a youngster due to my mother, a precious person. I give her a lot of credit. After entering the community and beginning to understand it and the Rule, I felt this was my way to virtue. The Rule is wonderful in its way of life. It gives a structure to live by. Whatever spirituality I have was gained through trying to follow the Rule. The solid structure of Benedictine life, especially the prayer life, has been so helpful to me. The Divine Office was very important to the community, and we were very conscientious about fulfilling it. We have now adapted our own prayer hours that fit our needs.

I appreciate the stability of the Rule and community living established in the Rule. This is part of my spirituality, and the Rule helps me to develop my own sense of spirituality. The prayer life established in the Rule is also very important to me.

We are a group of women living together. We have our pros and cons. We are physically very well cared for. We have a family-like relationship. In the Prologue of the Rule it gives you the message that if interested, come. If it's not for you, leave. It's so practical. The Rule calls for comfortable clothing that fits. It took us Vatican II and the change of habit to get back to the basics in Benedict's original thinking. It was difficult to change after all those years of dressing in the complex habit. It was tradition, but the Rule is flexible. There will be more ups and downs. There is no perfection. There will always be room for improvements.

I am hopeful that we in the community will continue to be what St. Benedict would want us to be. I hope we can be faithful to our community living and helpful to those who come to us, in whatever way we can, physically, mentally, or spiritually. I hope in the few years I have left that I can continue to be of help to others.

— Father —

JAMES JONES

Born 1924

Father James is a member of the Benedictine community at Conception Abbey in Conception, Missouri.

In the rolling farmland of Missouri, tucked away on a country road, are the tranquil grounds of Conception Abbey, founded in 1873. My elder is Father James, a former abbot here. I quickly find out he is quite a character. He often has a twinkle in his eyes, and seems to be having a bit of fun with me. When I ask him if he has any regrets about having chosen a monastic life his quick response is, "About three times a day." A droll smile slips across his face and he goes on to give me a more serious reply.

Often monastic life is idealized, and the Benedictines frequently remind me that nearly everything that goes on outside the monastery can also happen within. This point was driven home in a shocking way sometime after I had visited Conception Abbey. On June 10, 2002, at about 8:30 in the morning, a total stranger entered the abbey, unpacked two rifles, killed two monks, wounded two more, and then killed himself. But even in the midst of this great tragedy, the strength of Benedictine life was evident. The authorities asked the abbot, Gregory Polan, if he wanted the murderer taken to the morgue separately from the two monks. The abbot replied, "No, we are all God's children. They are going to the coroner together." Later, when he was asked how the shootings would change the abbey, Abbot Gregory's reply was a powerful example of Benedictine courage and forgiveness: "This has always been a place of welcome. We treat everyone as if she or he is Christ. For fifteen hundred years, Benedictine monks have welcomed people in that spirit. And we won't change."

Father James

I WAS BORN in Kansas City. My father was an attorney, and my mother was a college graduate as well. I was a rather spoiled only child and had a happy childhood. I went to parochial school in Kansas City. I graduated from elementary school at the age of twelve. My mother became ill with a brain tumor, and my father looked for a boarding school for me and found the Benedictine boarding school that was here at Conception Abbey. I came here as a high school freshman and was rather sad. I spent a lot of time in the big abbey church praying for my mother. She was later rediagnosed at the Mayo Clinic as not having a brain tumor and lived until the age of eighty-eight. After I had been here a year, my parents wanted me to come home, but I liked it here. I went for all four years of high school at Conception and received a really good education. We had five classes a day and four full hours of study hall. I then went to my first year of college at a Jesuit college in Kansas City. I had a great social life; I dated and had a good time. I also began to understand that I wanted to be a priest, but I wasn't sure what kind. I had a Jesuit spiritual father, and we discussed and prayed about becoming either a diocesan, Jesuit, or Benedictine priest. By the end of the year, he said he thought the Benedictines had it hands down, and that was the way I had always felt. So after one year in Kansas City, I returned to Conception for my second year of college. I entered the monastery at the age of eighteen. I really had no deep thoughts about spirituality, but I do remember that when I was in my first year of high school I wrote in my diary that in twelve years I would be a priest monk at Conception Abbey teaching first-year high school Latin. Twelve years later, I was doing just that.

When I joined, I spent a year in the novitiate, three years in simple vows, made solemn vows in 1946, was ordained a priest in 1948, and began teaching Latin in the high school and college. In 1949 the abbot called me in and said I was going to Rome to study. I had a grand time in Rome, received my master's in theology, came home and taught theology and Latin. After two years the abbot sent me back to Rome for a doctorate in canon law, which I received in three years. This is how monasteries worked in those days. I didn't like canon law. My daddy was a lawyer, but church law is very different. But the abbot said that is what I was going to study, and so I did. I spent the summers at Engelberg Abbey in Switzerland from which we were founded. Boy, that was heaven! The years in Rome were very joyful as I studied with men from thirty-six countries in that great historical setting.

When I came home in 1955, I was made subprior. As things worked out I served as subprior for ten years. Most of the time I was also teaching liturgical theology and canon law. In 1969–70 when I was dean of our school of theology, five Ph.D. monks left the community with the permission of the pope to get married. Well, they were good men and my good friends, but they left. You don't throw stones, but it was hurtful. In 1972, we had to give up our school of theology as the heart of the faculty was gone.

After that I became a hospital chaplain. In 1973, I was sent as chaplain to the Springfield federal prison. There I had my eyes opened. I was there four years. They were happy and difficult years. You were chaplain not only for the prisoners but also for their wives and the prison employees. Over half the inmates were black or Hispanic. I speak Spanish and celebrated a Spanish Mass once a week. When I first started at the prison, I decided to be more "modern" and wear a sports coat and tie some of the time. Well, this didn't go over big with the leader of the Italian inmate contingent. He requested a meeting with me, and I met with him and some of his men one afternoon after the count. They said they thought I was a fine priest, but they would like me to wear my collar and my black. They wanted me to look like a priest. It was an offer I couldn't refuse, and I agreed. From that time on there was no problem keeping that chapel full for each Mass. The problem was it was probably not for the right reason. At the rectory there were three other monks from Conception, and we would pray morning and evening Divine Office together and have a group dinner every evening. Without that I don't think I could have made it. My last two years working in the prison I was clinically depressed. I define depression as when everything becomes difficult to do. Tying your shoes is a big, difficult thing. I survived. Others helped me through. But I have been able to find some joy about everywhere I've been, even in prison.

In 1977, the thirty-six-year-old abbot of Conception chose me, then fifty-three years old, to be his prior. I was prior until 1987. That is a hard job, and I was teaching at the same time, but the time went very fast because I was so busy. The prior is an important man in a Benedictine monastery. The abbot makes the big decisions, but the prior makes all the arrangements of the monastery. You make an appointment to see the abbot, but you just bust in on the prior. The prior handles things such as weekend parish work designations for the priests, car assignments, and most of the daily working decisions of the abbey.

Then in 1987 our abbot was made a bishop, and I was elected abbot at the age of sixty-three. I truly cared for the men. Looking back, I don't think I was a very good abbot, but I worked hard and preached that our salvation was in our community life. It was a busy time. I did my best, but after six years at a meeting of abbots I noticed I was about the oldest abbot there. In spite of some objections, I resigned to make room for a younger man. I was then sent as senior priest to a parish in Kansas City. People babied me to death there, so after two years I returned to Conception, and I've been here ever since. I now work in the guest department here, and occasionally I give retreats around the country.

Prayer shapes our spiritual life at the monastery. We pray together six times a day for public prayer. We have private prayer. We have *lectio.* That is all I have ever known. I started that routine in high school. In those days I would even sneak into chapel between classes to have a few words with Jesus Christ. There are very few days since 1936 that I haven't been to daily Mass. My real Benedictine spiritual tradition started when I joined the novitiate at the age of eighteen. It's different with the diocesan priests, or Jesuits, or Franciscans, as their prayer is more on their own. We have communal prayer six times a day. Even when on mission work if there is a group of us, we keep up our group prayer together. The sisters are even better at keeping up their communal prayer when they are working away from their monastery. For that matter, the sisters are better than the monks!

The Benedictine life is a life of common people. We're not a bunch of very holy people, but we are trying. We're trying to serve.

Our physical life in the monastery is structured as well. You get up early. You eat well three times a day. You get some exercise. You get regular sleep. In my younger years, we had a tradition of recreation from 12:30 p.m. to 1:30 p.m. We had a handball court we built ourselves. There was one year, I think it was 1945, I played handball for 365 straight days.

In regard to the Rule of St. Benedict, Chapter 72 is of great importance. It begins by saying, "Just as there is a wicked zeal which separates from God and leads to hell, so there is a good zeal which separates from evil and leads to God and everlasting life. This, then, is the good zeal which monks must foster with fervent love. They should each try to be the first to show respect to the other, supporting with the greatest patience one another's weaknesses of body or behavior, and earnestly competing in obedience to one another." There may be brothers that I might not want to take a long vacation with. That's not the point. I have to understand and accept a brother's deficiency of character, and he has to suffer through mine. When I work with married couples on the verge of divorce, they sadly often don't seem to understand this. You see this on all levels of people's relations. The Rule asks us to deal with each other honestly. We need a good zeal, we need to respect and listen to one another. We shouldn't think that Benedictines are a bunch of angels. We fail all the time, but we do keep trying.

I see community as a primary Benedictine value. I see salvation in community, I see us living in a world community. Someone said that when anyone dies, a part of me dies. I can respect and accept the outside world.

Working in the guest department, we are to accept all people as Christ. That's easy for me, and it carries over into all my life. I think a lot of it goes back to my family. I had a magnificent mother and father. Their attitude toward others was the "good zeal." We had neighbors who were Baptists and Jews; they were all our friends.

Sometimes I think I would have liked to become the secretary of state. I'm proud to be an American and able to freely criticize my government, and I'm loyal to that. I think our foreign policy for the past twenty-five years or so has been largely wrong. For example, even Kissinger understood that we should recognize Cuba. We could wrap Castro around our little finger if we would treat him like a human being. Look at Nicaragua, Guatemala, Chile, and so much of our foreign policy.

I do have many hopes: hopes for this community, hopes for religion, and I wish I had hope for the country. More young people now do seem to be searching for the contemplative life. We have a program now during college spring break where college students, men and women, come to the abbey. We call it The Monastic Experience, and they really seem to like it. It's also cheaper than Fort Lauderdale.

I think that in the future we will remain a small community, which is fine. I'd like to see more students in the seminary. We have a fine small liberal arts school here.

My hope for our country is more a lament. I think our culture is in real trouble. Consumerism, the lack of values, the collapse of the family, these are all deep problems. I believe family is the heart of our society, and when statistics show that half of all marriages fail, we have many children suffering. That doesn't mean these kids are all damned or going to be failures, but they are going to suffer. This culture can't make it on this path.

I see hope for our monastery, I see hope for religion, but I have trouble having hope for our culture.

While I have no real regrets about having chosen the Benedictine life, one thing keeps nagging at me: that I should have been in the armed forces during World War II. I made a decision to go to the seminary in 1941 as I felt God was calling me. But I still wonder and have some regret.

I have never regretted being a Benedictine, but I remember once having regretted being prior. I sat down with Abbot Jerome, who was many years my junior, and said that I'd had it. I told him I'd been prior four or five years and I felt I wasn't getting anywhere and I thought I should get out. Abbot Jerome took me on a walk. He walked me up to the cemetery and said, "These are our successes. You will admit that every one of them that you knew were good men. They were faithful to the end. That's all we have to do — to keep our community together, faithful to Jesus Christ and the Father. So don't be so discouraged. Every one of these crosses is a victory." That made me feel good. They were all good guys who succeeded in life. They all had faults like you and me. They weren't canonizable saints, but they were real victories.

Sister

AUGUSTINE UHLENKOTT

1903–2002

Sister Augustine was a member of the Benedictine community at the Monastery of St. Gertrude in Cottonwood, Idaho.

❁

The Monastery of St. Gertrude is surrounded by rolling farmland and woods; mountains shine blue and violet in the distance. Blazing fields of yellow canola flowers greeted us as we drove up to the monastery. The main buildings have been built with native stone that the sisters helped haul down from the mountains in the 1930s. I was surprised to find a historical museum with a focus on Idaho history on the monastery grounds, as well as a rather diverse collection of Asian artwork and crafts, some dating back to the Ming Dynasty. Sister Augustine, my elder at the monastery, was well into her nineties at the time of our meeting. She had been almost eighty years at St. Gertrude's, including twelve years as its prioress. Now with her health failing and hearing nearly gone, she focused her life on prayer. "Although I don't have any special work to do," she said, "I do pray for each sister every day." Her work was *still very special indeed.*

Sister Augustine

When I was a child Benedictines surrounded me. All through the eighth grade I was taught by Benedictine sisters. My father had three sisters who were Benedictines, and my mother had one sister who became a Benedictine. My older sister also had become a Benedictine. We had all Benedictine pastors in our church. I simply couldn't do anything else. I always wanted to be a sister and a teacher, but I didn't want to be a teacher unless I could be a sister first. I grew up about three miles from St. Gertrude's. The influence of the church was very important. I felt that I needed to know if God really wanted me to be a sister. I told that to my mother, and she said that if I would be a good girl, God would let me know, and he did. I was living with two Benedictine sisters, helping them and doing some teaching. A priest was visiting for a retreat. I expressed to him, as I had to my mother, that I wanted to know if God wanted me to become a Benedictine. He said he would answer for my vocation and that I should go to the convent. That settled and started it. I went to the convent in 1920.

After my initial formation at the convent and two years of college at St. Scholastica in Atchison, Kansas, I was sent to teach elementary school, which I did for eight years. There was a group of five of us who lived in a house in Cottonwood, to be close to the school; it was a happy home. We taught two grades to a room at the school. Those were wonderful years. I also taught orchestra, glee club, and math in our high school for many years.

When I was fifty-two years old, I was elected prioress of St. Gertrude's for twelve years. During the last six years of my administration, I was also elected president of the fifteen convents of the Federation of St. Gertrude the Great. This was during the beginning of the Vatican II years. My term of office ended in 1967 when the experiments were starting. I was so much a part of the tradition of the Catholic Church that I found some of the changes difficult, and I was glad my time as prioress was ending. I had survived and had tried my best. I was then principal at our high school academy here for a time, and later I was sent to Boise where I taught piano for nineteen years at St. Mary's School. I retired when I was eighty-five. Although I'm not ill, I'm in the infirmary now. I do a lot of correspondence. I also handled the community donations for the missions for a long time. I do a lot of visiting of the sisters in the infirmary.

The greatest joy of my life would have to be when I took first vows, and my three years as a junior were all very happy. There were many joys teaching in the mission life. All my jubilee days have been wonderful; I've had six now: my twenty-five-year anniversary, fifty-year, sixty-year, sixty-five-year, seventy-year, and my seventy-five-year anniversary. There has been so much joy in just living with the sisters and being one myself. At one time we had twenty-one sisters joining us from Switzerland. I could speak German because we always spoke German at home. It just never seemed right to speak anything but German with my parents. However, with my brothers and sister I always talked English. The Swiss sisters just loved that I could speak with them in German. We have just three of them left now.

Even when we were living in groups teaching and doing mission work, we still tried to keep our sense of community living, even though we weren't in the monastery. We had our coordinator, or superior, and of course our common prayer. We always lived the Rule, and I think we sort of "Benedictinized" some of our students. The group of high school students who graduated from here fifty years ago came and held their reunion at the monastery not too long ago. One of the boys told me that after he graduated he really missed for many years hearing the sisters pray the Office. Praying this Office daily keeps me in touch with the whole praying church and the needs of the world.

Living the common life with our mission work embodies the values we live. The values that are the key to our life are clearly stated in Chapter 72 of the Rule, which speaks of the wicked zeal and the good zeal, and continues, "No monastics are to pursue what they judge better for themselves, but instead, what they judge better for someone else. Among themselves they show the pure love of sisters and brothers; to God, reverent love; to their prioress or abbot, unfeigned and humble love. Let them prefer nothing whatever to Christ, and may Christ bring us all together to everlasting life."

The common life and praying the Divine Office, which are summarized in our Benedictine motto, *ora et labora,* have been the foundation of my spiritual life. Daily reading of Scripture and the writings of Abbot Marmion have also influenced my spirituality.

The Prologue of the Rule of St. Benedict has always been very special to me. It begins with such tenderness: "Listen, my child, to my instructions, and attend to them with the ear of your heart. This advice is from one who loves you; welcome it and faithfully put it into practice. The labor of obedience will bring you back to God from whom you had drifted through the sloth of disobedience. This message of mine is for you, then, if you are ready to give up your own will, once and for all, and armed with the strong noble weapons of obedience do battle for Jesus, the Christ. . . ." Chapter 2 of the Rule on the qualities of the prioress or abbot was especially important to me during the years I had those responsibilities. It states clearly the responsibilities: "To be worthy of the task of governing a monastery, the prioress or abbot must always remember what the title signifies and act accordingly. They are believed to hold the place of Christ in the monastery. Therefore, a prioress or abbot must never teach or decree or command anything that would deviate from God's instructions. On the contrary, everything they teach and command should, like the leaven of divine justice, permeate the minds of the community. . . ."

The areas of the Rule on obedience and humility, charity, good relationships, and patience all have special meaning for me. The common or cenobite life in the love of Christ is shaped by the Rule.

I do have hopes for the future. In a way I'm very optimistic. I feel we have outstanding leadership in the church now. Our pope is such a wonderful, true leader. Regardless of criticism, he is outspoken and courageous. Thus the world can know what's right and what's wrong. He has a great influence in the world with his many travels and his special interest in the youth and values. In the Benedictine communities we are blessed with such wonderful, firm leadership. Our leaders practice what they preach. Their influence and the love they show reaches out beyond the community and touches others through their teaching and other mission work. There is hope for the future. We have been blessed with such fine leaders here too at St. Gertrude's, so Christ-like and so full of kindness, that I am confident that God will continue to bless our community.

Father

PLACID PIENTEK

Born 1918

Father Placid is a member of the Benedictine community at St. Andrew Svorad Abbey in Cleveland, Ohio.

❁

St. Andrew Svorad is an urban abbey, but one with well-designed buildings and lovely grounds, where one can quite easily forget that downtown Cleveland is only ten minutes away. But there are reminders of the surrounding city, like the pigeons that make for the abbey's primary "wildlife." Father Placid has been a city dweller most of his life, growing up on a street in New York City that later gave way to the World Trade Center.

Father Placid

I WAS BORN in New York City, in lower Manhattan in the shadow of Wall Street. I always wanted to be a priest. It was during the Depression and I needed to make a decision about schooling as I reached the eighth grade. I grew up in the Slovak parish attending a Catholic school taught by Slovak sisters. The Depression was very bad and many kids were quitting school, under the pretense of helping their parents make some money. I knew that wasn't for me. I asked one of the sisters what school she would recommend, and she sent me to the Slovak pastor, who said there were two Slovak possibilities: the first was St. Andrew Svorad in Cleveland, which was just starting out, and St. Procopius Abbey in Illinois. I chose Cleveland, and I think it was mainly because it was Slovak and because it was closer to New York and travel would be cheaper. I came here in 1932 at the age of fourteen. I began high school here and I really enjoyed it. My plans were to become a Slovak pastor and return to New York, but Father George, of happy memory, kept saying that I should become a Benedictine. In my fourth year I applied to the monastery. I admired their lifestyle. The Benedictines were active with us in our sports, conversation, and recreation — they were family. It was a very loving, wholesome environment. The funny thing was that Cleveland then sent me to study at St. Procopius, where I could have gone in the first place, for two years of college. After the two years there I was eligible for the novitiate. I was then sent to St. Benedict's in Atchison, Kansas, to finish my college education.

I completed my degree in Atchison in 1941 and returned to Cleveland. There were twenty-six seminarians here at that time. We started our own seminary, and I studied theology here for four years. I was ordained a priest in 1944. I then began teaching Latin, English, and religion at our high school here and also did quite a bit of coaching. I loved athletics. In 1948, I was appointed novice master. I spent all my life at the monastery except two years that I was sent to Rome to study as a novice master, from 1952 to 1954. After my time as novice master I returned to more teaching but also started with some administrative duties. I worked as treasurer at the high school and also at the monastery for some years. By 1969, I was doing full-time administrative work that continued for about the next twenty years.

I stepped down from the administrative work in the late eighties and focused on other work. I helped with our Slovak magazine for years. I help with mailings and fund-raising in various ways. I also help organize an annual volunteer dinner. It's become quite a beautiful event. It seems like everyone wants to come. A highlight of the dinner is a skit put on by the monks; one year the skit was titled "Holy Havana," and its plot was the pope asking the Benedictines to start a foundation in Cuba, and featured characters such as Jimmy Hoffa and Elvis Presley.

My whole life here has given me joy. I have been in vows for sixty years and every day has had a glow to it, not boring but growing. It's a thanksgiving to God that I am still here and able to work and pray for him. There has been no explosion of happiness but a steady constant union with God. I just keep growing at it, never tiring of it. I'm living under my fourth abbot here. It seems that each one keeps getting better. The current abbot is a godsend. He was one of my novices.

Of course there has been some sorrow. It has been sad to see some men leave the Benedictine life. They seem to be running away. It's also sad to see young men come and sample the life but still be afraid to make a real commitment.

I believe family life is a core value the world needs more of today. Now with both parents working and so many single-parent homes, it's very difficult. We are founded on the precept of the abbot being the father of the family, and he is elected for life. We could teach family values through the stability of our lives. We have a vow of stability that could help marriages and families stay together. The Rule also is very thoughtful about the old and the young; that could also benefit society today.

The Rule of Benedict has much guidance for us. I love the chapter on obedience and humility. It comes from the days I used to teach the chapters to the novices. I would try to teach them that humility and obedience are two sides of the same coin.

I've always seen the Prologue and the first seven chapters as the most important ones; after that, it's mostly details.

When I came here at the age of fourteen, I automatically became part of the spiritual practices of the Benedictines, and I have been part of that practice for the last seventy years. I began the Divine Office as a novice. The Office creates the rhythm of life with the seasons, the psalms, and the readings. It grows on you over the years. Even the changes from Latin to English didn't upset me. It seemed a normal growth. The Office is living. Even during the Easter season, when some reading might have as many as nine "Alleluias," you might think one or two would have been enough, but I like it with all nine. Some days we sing the Office rather than recite it.

You're happy with the embellishment, for the Office never gets boring.

The Benedictine way is a healthy, balanced way of life. You have all your companions helping you and guiding you. You go into the flow of things. They can spot it when you veer off the beaten path with food, exercise, or diet. And it's not just the superior helping you, but even more so the ordinary fellow monks. They encourage and help you to take care of yourself. It's wonderful the way it works with no beating of drums or fanfare, just genuine concern. Even in the later years there is always work to do. I always say Benedictines never retire. It's a family, and you want to continue to be part of it. The superior and other monks will never burden you with something beyond your capabilities or condition.

We don't have the concerns for security that so many people have when they grow older. We hear so much about planning for your retirement. That doesn't upset me because I don't have to worry about it. I don't need to worry about money or inflation or deflation. Those things are not concerns of my life.

I have hope for the future. I hope our monastery will grow. I hope we can return to the time we were more numerous. We have about forty members now, and at one time we were around seventy. Nature has many cycles and rebirths. Benedictines have their cycles and rebirths as well.

Sister

LIGUORI SULLIVAN

Born 1913

Sister Liguori is a member of the Benedictine community at Benet Hill Monastery in Colorado Springs, Colorado.

The beautiful Colorado Cliffs surround Benet Hill. The ochres, siennas, and umbers of the cliffs and the greens of the pines and firs create a vibrant environment. Benet Hill is very much a women's monastic community. It is thoroughly feminine: the modern chapel is filled with flowers; the liturgy has been modified to reflect the women who perform it with devotion and passion; the openness of their hearts is expressed in opening their facilities to the local Jewish and Buddhist communities.

When Sister Liguori enters the room for our first meeting, I can sense her presence beyond her physical appearance. An aura of quiet authority seems to surround her from her long years of administration on many levels. There is also a sense of pain—pain over the many changes she has undergone in her life and also the pain of her ailing health. But the pain is balanced and softened by her compassion. Her focus is not on herself but on others. Sister Liguori is a wonderful example of an individual who, through the love for others, can lessen, maybe even overcome her own struggle.

Sister Liguori

BEING INSPIRED by people who led Benedictine lives, some in spirit and others in reality, was a strong factor in my adolescent years when I was making decisions regarding my future. I grew up in Spring Fork, Missouri, and my parents, who were 100 percent Irish, and my three older sisters all gave me a deep reverence for the church. The only pastor I knew as a child, Father John Knoebber, was fifty years ahead of his time and instilled in me a love for a changing church. His two sisters were members of the Benedictine sisters at Mount St. Scholastica in Atchison, Kansas, and they impressed me. My oldest sister, Norine, entered Scholastica, and I attended the academy there, and these were contributing factors in my decision to follow a Benedictine life. While attending the academy I saw in action the basic prayer, community life, and ministry of the Benedictines. Mother Lucy Dooley was the prioress of the community of Mount St. Scholastica in 1933. She embodied for me all that a Benedictine leader should be: a balanced and moderate person, loving and with a sense of humor, and a judge between the trivial and essential things in life. I entered on June 12, 1933, was in formation as a novice one year and studied three years prior to my final profession of vows on January 1, 1938.

My parents had instilled a love for education and sacrificed much for the education of their children in the 1920s and 1930s. It seemed so right that my life duties should therefore be in the areas of teaching, administering, and founding schools. I taught in elementary and secondary schools, community college, and four-year liberal arts college. Organizing and directing a newly founded community college, secondary, and elementary schools has occupied much of my years of ministry. Donnelly Community College in Kansas City, Benet Hill Academy here in Colorado Springs, the John Neumann Catholic School in Pueblo, Colorado, and adult learning opportunity programs are all endeavors requiring great faith. Always I had great trust in, and support from, laypeople of experience and talent in founding these projects. These people were clearly direct gifts from God as life changed and my own limitations called forth their abilities. The John Neumann school is especially dear to me. A board of laypeople determining policies and supporting the operation has been unique but successful in that effort.

Living in a monastery, a spiritual place of prayer, plus pursuing a ministry, which has often focused on women, has made a great change in my attitude toward the outside world. First by listening to the stories of other women, I learned of their very great needs, of their oppressions and abuse. I have met their hurting eyes. Second, dealing with these needs has given me a greater compassion for others as they struggle just to survive. Third, besides lecturing with empathy, I learned to respond to needs by using my own gifts and energy to meet their needs. Fourth, I realized that my most-often-said prayer, "God, you are my strength, you are my song," has an infinite source of strength to supplement my own. And that is the reason for the success of the adult learning programs which I direct.

Each morning as I walk around the campus on the way to our chapel, I thank God for the holy ground given us. I pray that it will always house holy people and be the place of holy work. Seeing God in everything, every person, and every event is important. An abiding sense of the sacred must be strong.

Once chosen, our fidelity to religious life has to be maintained and we must allow it to grow stronger. Never can it remain dormant, or it will diminish and we will not be able to bring religious life to others. Some believe our vows should be changed in name from the age-old — poverty, chastity, and obedience. The semantics may seem antiquated but down deep they carry the message of seeking God. If they are lived with fidelity through the years, we may be able to say, "I have sought God, and found him." Connotations of these values may change over the centuries, and rightfully so, but the essence of seeking God always remains the same.

While the Rule of St. Benedict advances no methods, no set forms, it does devote many chapters to common prayer solidly based in Scripture and nurtures a deep love of the gospels. The Rule creates a foundation for my spiritual life. Reverence for all creation from the smallest to the greatest became formative. This was further enriched with the spirituality of Teilhard de Chardin in merging the sacred and the secular. The awareness of the presence of God in all events of living has grown very steadily in my life. The saying "Life is a circle" has made the family rosary a contemplative prayer now that I am an elder Benedictine and deeply enmeshed in the gospel. The power of common prayer can sometimes overwhelm me as I wonder, "How can prayer be answered so quickly?" The answer is, "Why shouldn't it be?" The *opus Dei,* the work of God, is our foremost ministry.

The sense of a sacred community of persons, which is an integral part of Benedictine life, has always been of special significance to me. Perhaps having been born as the youngest member of a closely knit family where I was nurtured by uncles, aunts, and dozens of cousins as well as my immediate family, perhaps living in a small country parish where I was guided by a loving pastor, attending a grade school of less than thirty pupils, perhaps all this prepared me for community living. I am not hermitical in nature!

The Rule teaches us to seek God as a group. We worship and praise God together in prayer. We share our strengths and weaknesses in varied ministries. We thrive and grow as a community or we diminish and die as one. We respect the individuality of each other. All this adds up to knowing love for each other, which is the bond that holds all things together, stretching up from atomic particles to the Trinity itself.

The regularity and moderation found in Benedictine tradition dictate the way I live my physical life and enable me to employ the limited energy which I have. Scheduling for common worship and prayer is important. Benedict understood the need for a nap! He urged consideration for the elderly. I had perfect health until 1945. Since then it has been a series of cancers, surgeries, illnesses, and treatments. My history of physical suffering has been a mystery in my life. Grounding in Jesus' words, "I came to do the will of my Father," has helped me accept the mystery and value of all suffering since he chose suffering. To know it as part of our evolutionary creation is strengthening to my acceptance of it as well.

Benedictine moderation in food, sleep, and work all contribute to a sense of well-being needed to live a common life and to contribute my share to "living by the work of our own hands." The sanctity of work is important to me.

My awareness of the presence of God in every person, place, and event ranks first among many joys in life. A sense of being part of a community life, from my childhood to the present, whether that was my religious group, my classroom, my school, my ministries, even my supportive board members, all have given me great joy. Seeing the eyes of children, of youth, and of adults light up when learning comes to them is a joy for me. This learning can be of all good truth with no secular or sacred division, but I know that all learning can lead to the one who said, "I am the Truth." To know that we can be a part of this process is a source of great joy.

With these many joys must come some sorrows. Because the ministry of education in all its shapes and forms has been so important in my life, I find myself grieving when children are exposed to evil by educative measures wherever they are used. This ranges from the home itself to the most sophisticated of our media. Innocence can never be known by the younger generation of today.

On the cosmic level, our failure to accept responsibility as co-creators of the earth is a great sorrow. Our great and beautiful earth, "ever ancient, ever new," is threatened and we do little to prevent it.

I am also saddened to live in our beautiful country while it has turned into a genocidal society. From prebirth to death, our genocidal policies regarding the sanctity of life is not only imposed in our country but also imposed on other countries helpless in their poverty. Our challenge is to change this and in doing so to reassure ourselves that "God is still in charge."

My greatest hope for the cosmos is that we may be an active element in preventing the genocide which threatens our world. The flow of life is so precious, and women are the determiners of victory!

My greatest hope for the future is identical with the hope I had in 1963 when seventy of us said yes to creating the community of Benet Hill. God was "our strength and our song" then and now. By remaining true to the charisma of the past, but living in the present, we make the changes which have the life of the future embedded in them. There is a famous line, "Let there be no moaning when we put out to sea." In a sense that is the present time we share with thousands of other religious. There may be times when we are called to give ourselves to ministries other than those we chose. At those times we must accept the challenges.

Father

PAUL R. MAHER

Born 1925

Father Paul is a member of the Benedictine community at St. Vincent Archabbey in Latrobe, Pennsylvania.

❁

Approaching St. Vincent Archabbey, I am aware that I am about to visit the "granddaddy" of them all — the first Benedictine abbey in the United States. It was founded in 1846 by Boniface Wimmer, whose biography is an enjoyable portrait of a very multifaceted man. He arrived in America with eighteen men, and at the time of his death he had created five abbeys administering 152 parishes with over four hundred monastic members. I am to meet with a retired archabbot of the abbey, Father Paul. I expect him to be a modern-day version of Boniface Wimmer, and I'm a little bit anxious. My anxiety is gone as soon as I meet Father Paul. He is a very intelligent, highly experienced abbot who also has the demeanor, gentleness, and openness of an ideal parish priest.

Father Paul

I'M FROM a large family right here in Latrobe. I'm the ninth of eleven children, and a number of us found religious vocations. One of my brothers became a diocesan priest, and one of my older sisters joined the Sisters of Mercy. I had the example of my older siblings. I went to a parish school and became an altar boy. I was thinking vaguely even at a young age about the possibility of becoming a priest. I received a scholarship to attend the prep school that was here at St. Vincent at the time as a day student. That was very fortunate, as there was no way we could have paid the tuition. The prep school was my first contact with Benedictines, and as I went through my four years of school I began to see that the Benedictine life was a good way of living. I found it attractive, and I began to think about a Benedictine priesthood.

I finished high school in 1943 in the middle of World War II. Four of my older brothers were in the army. I had the option of going to the seminary here at St. Vincent, but I still was not sure enough to take that step. Two months after I turned eighteen, I was in the army. I ended up in the air force as a B-24 tail gunner. I flew twenty-one missions over southern Germany and Austria and was discharged in 1945 with the end of the war.

By now I had decided that I should give a religious vocation a try. I knew if I didn't I would spend the rest of my life wondering if I should have been a priest. I knew St. Vincent was where I wanted to make the attempt. I entered school here in 1946, joined the novitiate in 1947, made first vows in 1948, became a cleric student for the priesthood, and took solemn vows in 1951.

After receiving my bachelor's degree and one year of theology study at St. Vincent, I was sent to Rome to study. There I studied theology and received a Ph.D. in philosophy. I was ordained a priest in 1953 at the tomb of St. Francis in Assisi and finished my studies in Rome in 1957. I returned to St. Vincent and began teaching, and living in a student dormitory as a moderator. After three years of teaching I was also named socius of clerics, in charge of the junior monks. In 1963, I was appointed vice-rector of the seminary.

In 1966, I was sent to Taiwan as superior of a small priory we have there. We taught at a Catholic university in Taiwan. There were such huge changes in the late 1960s. When I went to Taiwan, I did not return for my first visit for four years. When I did return, it was quite a shock. Many reforms of Vatican II had been instituted, and there was such a change in the students in the college — they were barefoot, longhaired, and bearded — quite a change from the military uniformed students we had in Taiwan. But many of the changes that took place were good and much needed.

In 1983, when I was home at St. Vincent for a routine summer visit, I was elected archabbot. As abbot my goal was to enable individual monks to best use their gifts and talents; when that worked and I could see it happening in the monk and within the community, it was very satisfying. It is rewarding to see a young man come as a novice and get a feel for where he is at that time and then watch him evolve academically, monastically, and spiritually. It may almost be like a married couple watching one of their kids grow up. Our contact comes later in life, but there is still so much growth that takes place. I also sometimes had sadness as an abbot when my enabling approach did not work — when the growth of an individual did not take place. It is difficult to see people leave the community, especially when you had great hopes for them, but sometimes it just doesn't work out.

I was archabbot from 1983 to 1990. I retired in 1990 with the understanding that I did not wish to be considered for reelection. I then worked at one of our parishes for five years and returned to the monastery in 1996 as head guestmaster.

I can truthfully say that I don't have any regrets in having chosen a Benedictine life. Occasionally one does have fleeting thoughts about "what if?" But I've never had serious regrets. I've actually been puzzled by the occasional monk who does express regret. Yes, I have had a few frustrations, but those frustrations have never been able to touch the basic peace and contentment that this monastic life has given me. Even within my field of study, philosophy, I'm no great philosopher, but I have greatly enjoyed the study and teaching of the subject. I can think of no great disappointments in my life, but then you are probably not going to find many Benedictines with great disappointments — if they had them they have already left. I'm very happy as a Benedictine priest, but I do think I could also have been happy as a diocesan priest.

Even as a student, I was attracted to what I saw as the balanced life of the Benedictines. It seemed a Catholic life of teaching, preaching, even grounds work. It was a healthy life. After joining the Benedictines, this balance of prayer and work became even more evident, and the moderation and humaneness of the life became more focused. I grew up as what you could call a ghetto Catholic. It was always around me, it was my environment. The Benedictine tradition was a kind of continuation of that.

Good health is part of the lifestyle. We have three good meals a day and good health care. I enjoy walking. I also enjoy my sleep, and I've often said the biggest sacrifice of my joining the monastic life is having to get up early in the morning. I enjoy good health. We have a relaxed lifestyle and freedom here at St. Vincent that I very much appreciate.

When Vatican II came with its emphasis on renewed liturgy and Scripture, I felt that we as Benedictines were already halfway there to the reforms being enacted. It wasn't a dramatic, jarring change for us.

The community of prayer in the choir of the Divine Office is the heart of my prayer life. Like many others are, I am occasionally bored and distracted in group prayer, but still the nourishment is there. My private prayer life is based on *lectio.* My *lectio* may be a bit more casual than some. I read Scripture commentary and theology that leans toward the academic as part of my *lectio.*

Within our community we try to be open to the outside world, some might say too open. In the area of hospitality we are to receive guests as if we were receiving Christ. Our education emphasis here at St. Vincent necessarily involves interaction with the outside world. We have many parishes connected to the monastery, and some are pretty far flung. We have one as far away as Virginia Beach, Virginia, about five hundred miles away. We have been doing some pulling back from parish work out of necessity. In the sixties, we had about 270 men in the community. We now have fewer than 200, 15 of whom are in our priory in Brazil, and the number continues to decrease.

❁

The values that motivate our work are the love of God and love of our neighbor. More specifically and within the Rule, hospitality is a very important value for us. Hospitality must be shown not just toward guests but toward our students and all others we have contact with, even though there are times when it might be difficult to treat all students as Christ.

Prayer and work are two key Benedictine values that are both tied to community life and the application of family values to our community. In my years as abbot, I tried to reinforce these values through day-to-day decisions and attempting to cultivate an atmosphere conducive to these values rather than preaching or holding a lot of conferences for the monks.

The Rule of St. Benedict forms the foundation of our life. There are parts and sentences from the Prologue through the chapters where the moderation and humaneness of Benedict comes through that have a special significance for me. These are the qualities of the Rule that make it so viable and are part of the reason that it became the standard rule throughout Europe for monastic orders. Charlemagne actually tried to impose the Rule on his empire, and it did become the standard, but through a kind of osmosis rather than imposition.

There are so many little human touches in the Rule, such as Benedict's provision that monks in his day could not get along without wine so he provides a beaker a day for each. Even in the areas of discipline where the abbot is punishing a monk by not being allowed at the table or prayer, Benedict says that several of the older monks should go to the one being punished and console him. There is so much gentleness and moderation in the Rule, and underlying it all is a firm scriptural basis.

One aspect of Benedictine monasticism that is more or less taken for granted today is the scholarly nature of many monks. The basis for that tradition cannot really be found in Benedict's Rule. It is part of our tradition that some historians trace back to Cassiodorus, who had a monastery in southern Italy and was a contemporary of Benedict. He saw as his main work having his monks copy manuscripts. This was the beginning of the tradition of the scriptorium. The main thrust of European monasticism became a combination of Benedict's Rule and Cassiodorus's scholarly tradition.

My hopes for the future focus on development. Some of my hopes are to see development and growth in the monastery, the church, society, and the world. I hope that Benedictine life and St. Vincent will flourish. I don't know how realistic that is in our day and age, but the flourishing may be in spiritual quality rather than in numbers. I hope that flourishing will not be just in our monastery but within the church as a whole. Within that general flourishing, I hope that individual monks will also grow and develop in terms of Christian humanism, by which I mean in the Benedictine sense growing in God-centered lives, not rejecting the world but transforming society, the world, and ourselves. Christian humanism differs from secular humanism in that, in the secular form, humankind is placed at the center, but in Christian humanism God is at the center and his creation is good.

Sister

AGATHA BURKE

Born 1920

Sister Agatha is a member of the Benedictine community at St. Joseph Monastery in Tulsa, Oklahoma.

St. Joseph's may not have the pastoral charm of some of the rural monasteries I am visiting, but it brims with the energy and dynamics of an urban monastery, administering a thriving preschool through middle school of twelve hundred students. Sister Agatha is the perfect representative of the institution. As our conversation evolves, I find myself thinking how wonderful it would have been had my children been her students, or if my young grandson could be. I feel that she embodies all the love and intelligence one could ever hope for in a teacher of young people.

Sister Agatha

WHEN I WAS six years old, I was baptized a Catholic so I could attend a new Catholic school here in Tulsa that was just opening. My father was a Catholic, but my mother was not. I remember at my baptism, a nun came out of the sacristy. It was the first time I had ever seen a sister and I was startled, but I kept watching her. There was something special about her. She seemed somewhat angelic through my eyes as a child.

I then attended that Benedictine school for twelve years. I admired and loved the sisters very much. I found my vocation by observation and association with them. I had a desire to join them, as I could see all the good things they did for people. I could see their love and dedication to the children. They taught so thoroughly that you couldn't help but learn. We lived just across the alley from the school, and I would spend a lot of time at the school doing little chores for the sisters and grew very attached to them. My mother did oppose my becoming a sister. She had become a Catholic herself but still did not like the idea of my joining a community. I postponed joining the order for five years after graduation as we were at war at that time and my brothers were all gone. I needed to be home to help the family. When I did go to the monastery, my mother practically disowned me. I had no correspondence with her, but my father would write to me. She did come when I received the habit, and when she saw how happy I was, she apologized for trying to stop me from coming. When she went home, she told all her friends that she couldn't believe that I could be that happy. She thought that if I went and was not happy, they would force me to stay. Of course, that was absolutely incorrect, as they advise you to leave if you're not happy.

I was a postulant for one year, a novice for one year, and in simple vows for three more years. We studied at our motherhouse in Guthrie, Oklahoma, and I received my bachelor's degree from there. I later received my master's degree in elementary education with a minor in administration from Catholic University in Washington, D.C. I've taught kindergarten through intermediate grades. I was principal of schools for twelve years. My mother, who was still here in Tulsa, became ill and was confined to a wheelchair. The community allowed me to go and take care of her. When I went, I didn't think she would live very long, but I guess it was the loving care she received, for I was with her seven years. She was so happy that I could be with her, she said she never would have guessed that it would be me who would take care of her in her old age. God is good. After she passed away, I then returned to the community full-time.

Our preschool through middle school here, Monte Cassino, is doing very well. We have about twelve hundred students. Only about six sisters teach there, and the administrator is also a sister. The rest of the staff is laypeople. We have excellent teachers. Many teachers would rather work here than in the public school, as we have discipline here. We require the children to respect the teachers, and in turn the teachers respect the children. We have a wonderful relationship with the parents of our students, who are very interested in their children's education. Another sister and I run an after-school program for the students who need to stay until their parents can pick them up. We have about 160 students and ten assistants.

I also served as secretary for the monastery for some y and served one term as subprioress. I also served on council of our Federation for three years.

The happiest day of my life was when I received the ha I knew I had reached the goal of giving my life back to G Each step along the way has been a time of great joy: first vows, my final vows, the celebration of twenty-five ye in the community, and the celebration of fifty years in community.

The joy of working with people and children in partic lar has been wonderful. Working with small children is li working with flowers. You work with them, such as teachi them to read, and they just open up. It's so beautiful to watc There is so much excitement in them. It is a true joy to b part of that.

Life has had some sorrows as well. There was much sorro in the loss of my parents and in the loss of my brothers. Whi I know they are now happier and better off, it is still sad see them pass.

There was also sadness in another kind of loss — the lo of members of the community, especially when a group sisters left us in the late sixties to start a new community. was hard to experience the loss of people who had been a pa of your life and then were no longer there. But God took ca of us, and we are continuing and so are they.

Our motto is prayer and work, and that takes first place in life. Everything flows from our prayer life. The Divine Off done as a community morning, noon, and evening, combin with our private prayer and the daily Eucharist, creates a

of prayer. Only illness keeps us from this schedule. Our prayer life is so much a part of us that we take it everywhere with us — inside us. It becomes a part of all our interaction with the people we are serving. In working with children, our work is a prayer. Children are handled in a loving, cheerful way. Through your example you try to bring Christ to them. You show them that God is a loving God who cares for them. We try to show them that they need not fear God, that he is a loving Father who is there to help us help them.

The prayer life as spelled out in the Rule has much meaning to me. The family structure designed in the Rule with a superior over us who takes the place of Christ is very important to me. The Rule's emphasis on love, respect, and obedience is at the heart of our community.

We study the Rule very thoroughly in the novitiate and we continue to read it daily at our evening prayer. There is always something new to be found in it. St. Benedict was truly a wise man. It is the way of our life.

Our physical life involves our work, and we try to be mindful that we are doing God's work and not ours. We try to be available and serve people in any way we possibly can. One of the things many people ask us to do for them is to pray for them in times when they are in need. We enroll them in our apostolate prayer, and we pray for them each day.

Even our physical appearance is part of the tradition. After Vatican II gave communities more freedom in the choice of clothing, we agonized over the right decision. As a community we came to the determination to always wear black and white and to keep the veil. It could be called a simple habit. When we travel people often come to us and ask us to pray for them or tell us that it's so good to see a sister in a veil. If we didn't have the simple habit, these people wouldn't even know we were

sisters. People will often come to you and ask advice because they can see who you are. It gives you an opportunity to try to bring Christ to these people. Being visible makes a difference.

Regarding our physical life, we have very wholesome, balanced meals, as prescribed by the Rule, and the best health care possible. We are blessed with doctors in the city who help our community in any way they can. Here at the monastery we have a health center with nurses' aides around the clock for the older sisters who live there. They get excellent care.

I feel we need to pray much for people in the outside world and their needs. We need to reach out to them whenever we can and in any way that we can.

As a community we have love for the poor and try to do what we can to help them. Many of our sisters help Catholic Charities in the summer in their food and clothing programs for the poor. We have volunteered our time for programs for unwed mothers and victims of AIDS as well. We also try to instill a sense of charity in the students we teach with various programs.

We try to see situations with the eyes that Jesus would like us to have. We try to think of how he would treat those in need. We try to be an instrument of his hands. We hope we can bring people to Christ through our prayers and example.

Respect for human life and the help and support we can give to people in physical and spiritual need are very important values for us. Also the value of our relationship to God and how we maintain that and attempt to share that with those outside of our life are key values. Our life is the value of service to each other and the world.

I hope the Lord will send young women to us so we can be strengthened and renewed. I hope our numbers will be maintained so we can continue to do what is asked of us by our Lord and the church. I believe that there are many young women out there who are just as generous as we were when we came to religious life. I believe we are in a time of waiting, and they will come. God's work needs to go forward, and they will have to do it when we are gone. I believe there will always be a need for the work we do and that God will provide for it. We have a lot of young women looking at us, but it seems to be a spirit of our time that people are afraid of commitment. You see it in marriages as well. This will eventually have to right itself, and I think it will. It's my hope and prayer that generous young women can make a covenant for life.

I hope that our community will always be of service. It may be that we will not always be teachers. God may have other things for us to do, and that's fine. But I do feel sure that he will always need our services in some way.

Father

FREDERIC SCHINDLER

1921—1999

Father Frederic was a member of the Benedictine community at Mount Michael Abbey in Elkhorn, Nebraska.

The brown and golden colors of early spring framed Mount Michael Abbey as I drove up to it through the suburban sprawl of Omaha, which increasingly encroaches on the once-rural monastery. Mount Michael's primary mission is its Benedictine High School for Boys, a venture that keeps most of its monks quite busy. Father Frederic had spent his share of time teaching, along with a host of other duties, but now he was very emphatic that I needed to see his new lawn mower which he used as the monastery's groundskeeper. During my meeting with Father Frederic, it became clear that the depth of his devotion and spiritual insight was extraordinary, but I also felt something else. It was a warmth and openness of the human heart I had never as consciously experienced before. I began to understand that in Father Frederic, I had found the genuine, unconditional love as taught by Jesus.

Father Frederic

I WAS BORN in the sand hills of Nebraska, and later grew up in Elgin, Nebraska. When I look back on where I came from and where I have been, my life seems to be an act of God's providence. There is no other way to explain it. I do think he leads every person.

There was no presence or sign of Benedictines from where I came. We once had a mission priest, a Dominican, I think, who gave a series of talks in our parish, and they were so down-to-earth. I've always had a yearning to listen to sermons. Our local pastor who had been in our parish since I was two or three years old was exemplary, truly a priestly man. Early on I had the feeling that it would be nice to be like him. I later mentioned to him that I was interested in the priesthood. Arrangements were made for me to go to college at Conception Abbey in Missouri.

We were so poor during those Depression years. The drought years with the dust storms and grasshoppers were a terrible time. Those kinds of conditions made me think of very basic questions, like, "What is life really all about?" My family raised no objections regarding my desire to become a priest. They tried to help me as much as they could. We were a close-knit family. I did get very homesick when I left home, and homesickness stayed with me off and on until I was ordained. I still dearly love to be with my brothers and sisters. It's something very deep. In trying to live the life of Benedict, you begin to see the value of people and especially those close to one's self. The Benedictine life has enhanced my love for others.

In 1938, I went to Conception Abbey to study. During my first two years at college, I stayed with the Benedictine sisters at Clyde, working for my room and board. I walked back and forth daily to school at Conception, a distance of two miles. In those two years, I got well acquainted with the Benedictines. After getting to know the way of life of both the monks and the nuns, I had no problem in deciding that the Benedictine life was the right direction for me. I entered the novitiate at Conception and after a year made simple vows. Three years later, I made final vows.

I was ordained a priest in 1945, and shortly thereafter began teaching Latin and English in the high school at Conception Abbey. Then, out of the blue, the abbot asked me to go to the American Indian mission in North Dakota. I was up at Fort Yates on the Standing Rock Reservation for three years. I loved it up there. The people and the open spaces were wonderful. At first I was somewhat in awe of the Indians as Native Americans. They have their own traditions and culture. We had a little farm in connection with the mission church and school. We raised a lot of our own food, both for ourselves and for the children attending the school. I had two small mission churches for which I was responsible. One was twenty-five miles upstream on the Missouri River at Cannonball. The second was seventeen miles downstream in South Dakota, just above Mobridge at Kenel. Both original missions are now underwater, due to the flooding of the river by the Oahe Reservoir.

One day I received a letter in the mail from Abbot Stephen, whereby he appointed me as chaplain to the Benedictine Sisters of Perpetual Adoration at Clyde, where I had lived and worked for two years as a student. So I returned to Missouri and was chaplain there for nine years. The sisters lead an intense religious life. At that time they maintained a twenty-four-hour adoration of the Blessed Sacrament. Their dedication made a deep impression on me. One of my duties was having religion classes for the younger sisters in formation. Some of the nuns at Clyde had been in the convent for fifty or sixty years. They had developed a deep understanding of things of God. They might not have had all the theological terms, but when it came to understanding the wisdom of God, I stood in admiration of those nuns. As is often the case, it's not the theologian who is the saint, but the people who have come to know God in prayer, to love him and live by his will. That is where you find the image of God beautifully exemplified. The sisters' beautiful chapel, their manner of life, and the immaculate cleanliness of their home and of their surroundings were a marvelous expression of their faith.

I was then appointed novice master at Conception Abbey and held that assignment for two years. Then, in 1964, the abbot sent me here to Mount Michael, and I've been here ever since. I began teaching Latin in the minor seminary and eventually taught German. I am presently oblate director for our oblates. They are a wonderful group of people. They are lay members affiliated with the community. They study the Holy Rule and try to apply its gospel to their own lives, whatever their vocation, the best they can.

I am also the groundskeeper. I've always worked outside when it was possible. We recently got a new mower. It might be called the Cadillac of mowers, and it does such a nice job of keeping the grounds neat and trim. On weekends, we priests go to various parishes in and around Omaha to help with pastoral duties. Several times each month, I am assigned as confessor to sisters' communities in Omaha.

❁

I have tried not to be conformed to the outside world. The spirit that I have been describing is radically opposed to the predominant spirit of the outside world. There is God's way, and there is man's way. They are opposites. You cannot serve two masters. That is not to say that all in the world is bad. God created it and it is good. But it is the worldliness that is so contrary to God's will. It leads to a denial and separation from God. Confusion and despair are the result.

"Vanity of vanities. All is vanity," we read in Holy Scripture. Benedict knew the world for what it was and fled from the corruption of Rome to his hermitage to seek God. "Do you seek God?" is what Benedict asks of everyone who comes seeking entrance into the community. This must be the purpose of one's coming; otherwise the Rule will not work. If you have come to the monastery for some secondary reason, such as avoiding the difficulties of making a living in the world, or for social prestige, you will be a misfit. You will do harm to yourself and be a burden to others. One must truly seek God. If Benedict were here today with all the social ills in society, I think he would probably flee again to a hermitage.

A joy in my life is doing what God expects of me, or at least trying to do so. The joy of doing God's will, as hard as it may be at times, may not always be on the front burner. But true obedience does bring contentment and deep satisfaction. You know you can never fully achieve God's expectations, but at least making the effort brings satisfaction. None of us attains full perfection in this world, but one's perfection, I think, is in the striving.

Another joy is being appreciated and respected by one's fellow monks, this in spite of one's failings and unworthiness. It is heartwarming to have others accept you and regard you as one of the monastic family.

Prayer, *lectio,* and time for quiet reflection are a great help for me to find peace with God. These elements bring one to a knowledge and experience of God. To know God's mercy and compassion in connection with his love brings a deep sense of trust, and this trust is the foundation of one's peace and security for the future. With a deep trust in God's love, mercy, and compassion, the sharp edge of the fear of death is removed.

One of the hardest things that has come my way in life was when I left home, my parents, brothers, and sisters to study for the priesthood. But in spite of this burden, deep down in my heart, I never wavered in my resolve. At the time I entered the monastic community, there was a policy of never returning home. This too made itself felt. But God's grace was present to strengthen and guide. This was especially evident, I think, at times of my making solemn vows and at my ordination. One might think these would be occasions for a joy ride, but they were not. They were times of a deep sense of apparent abandonment by God. And yet, now I see those occasions as signs of God's presence and special care. Could it have been that God as the potter was fashioning the vessel?

Now after almost sixty years of monastic life, a sadness arises from an awareness of how many people in the world live without a sense and a knowledge of God and of what the purpose of life is. So many seem to be unaware why they are on this earth and drift through life aimlessly. If they could only see and experience the things that we monks see and experience in our dedication as monks! God is wonderful in his gifts.

Another sorrow arises from my own sinfulness, weakness, and especially for times of ingratitude. When I think back over my life, there have been so many lost moments that could have been spent in a deeper awareness of God. The preciousness of time makes one realize that so much remains yet to be done, and the time is growing short. May our Blessed Lord make up for lost time in my regard and fill the void with his abundance. Hopefully, he will bless me with the grace of the worker in the vineyard who came at the eleventh hour.

The basis of our spiritual life is life in community based upon the principles of the gospel. It is a family life with a lasting commitment. You make a promise to live for life with this particular group of men. They truly become brothers to you. You know them, and they know you. We learn to take one another as we are. That is important in learning to live the gospel. There is not much room for sham. One of the basic problems people have is pride. The family life is like a medicine. It engenders a life of humility. Your brothers, as well as the abbot, know both your weaknesses and your strengths.

The Benedictine community or family is structured to help one seek God. It isn't a rarefied search that might lead to discouragement. Rather it is a search wherein you have many brothers ready to help one another along the way. The search grows naturally out of the way you live. Benedictine asceticism is simply incorporated in monastic life itself. There is self-denial in learning to put up with one another. You learn to respect not only each other but also your surroundings and all that is part of your life.

Our life of prayer is a principal element in Benedictine spirituality. When we assemble in prayer, we form the mystical body of Christ. Then it is Christ who is praying and Christ who is singing. It is only Christ who can really adequately glorify and honor the Heavenly Father. Benedict understood this and dedicated eight chapters of the Rule to the Divine Office.

Benedict does not have much to say about private prayer. For private devotion, Benedict recommended private meditative reading, *lectio*. *Lectio* is comprised mainly of reading the Holy Scripture. And the Scriptures are read not simply to gain information but with the awareness that the Word of God is the voice of God. It is a conversation with God. Then we are to reflect and contemplate God's presence and listen to what he is saying to us. It is a deep enhancement of one's spiritual life.

Benedictines are called "regulars" according to canon law. That means we are people who follow a rule. In our lives it is the regularity that is so conducive for a healthy physical life. Things are pretty much the same every day—prayer, meals, rest, and work all balance. There is the saying that "Grace builds on nature." I believe that if things are harmonized in the physical, it has a very important bearing on the spirit.

Finding the correct balance is important. One doesn't want to be a workaholic, nor a slacker. It reminds me of a story about Pope John XXIII. A reporter once asked him how many people worked at the Vatican. To which he answered with a twinkle in his eye, "About half of them."

For Benedictines, work itself is a praise of God. Human beings with intelligence and the ability to make, form, and create things are in a way a participation in God's creative work. To make things of beauty reflects God's reality. He is the Supreme Beauty. We try to keep our buildings, grounds, and surroundings clean and neat because it says something. It says something about God's kingdom.

We have developed a soft rhythm of life. One aspect of our lives flows from another. It becomes a life of habits that develop the sweetness of the Lord. It has not been a life without difficulties. There have always been up and down times. The mercy of God is such, however, that there is no time we can't turn to him for help. I think of difficulties and disappointments as a pruning knife in the hands of a loving Father. The Father is always interested in more fruit.

Our primary value in the monastery is faith. Monasticism is a life of faith. Without it, our life makes no sense. By faith, we enter into the world of God. Faith leads to prayer, and prayer is absolutely essential to our way of living. Prayer is not just the reciting of words but the deep interior communion with God that rises from the depths of the heart. Prayer is a yes to God. In prayer, one becomes aware of God's presence everywhere and in all things. All becomes sacred with this awareness. God's act of creation is continual. We and everything around us are present due to God's creative hand. If we understand this, we see the sacredness of nature and our own God-given dignity.

This brings us to a sense of the sacredness of work. Work is a gift of God. It's not meant to be an ordeal but something that fulfills us. In God's image we, in a sense, renew God's work with our talents and creativity. We have the capacity to enhance creation and give expression to God's creative presence. In this way others can come to a knowledge of the reality of God and his goodness.

Another essential element in monastic life is having a deep respect for others. Being created by God and called to baptism, we are all children of God. As God's children we come to respect one another. This is an echo of the reverence we have for God. As our Lord has told us, "Love one another as I have loved you." Then the respect and reverence we have for one another extends to all things of the monastery. St. Benedict admonishes us that the tools of the monastery are to be honored as though they were the sacred vessels of the altar. God's creation is all gift. As St. Paul puts it, "What hast thou that thou hast not received?" Everything that God has created is on loan to us. This is true of all nature, of our own bodies and souls, our talents. We need to use them and invest them well.

The Rule of St. Benedict is so remarkable. Benedict was not a theologian. But the Rule is not man's work alone. Benedict was God's creation, and through his Holy Rule he speaks with a deep awareness of God and a taste for the things of God. The Rule drinks deep from the well of the Scriptures. In fact there are more than five hundred quotations or allusions to the Holy Scripture in the Rule. Benedict didn't write the Rule because he saw the need for it in the ages to come, but rather he wrote it to fill the need at his time, for poor people who came to him for help. So he put into writing a few things, and now it continues to be this marvelous living document created fifteen hundred years ago. The only way to explain the Rule is that Benedict had a special charism from God. The Rule is oriented to individuals living in community. It deeply reflects God's love for humankind and for each human person. Scripture says we are created in God's own image. That says a lot. The gifts that we have, the power to know, the power to choose, to be free, to be responsible, all reveal humankind's great dignity and worth. When God came as a man he didn't come for the powerful or the rich. He came for the poor, the weak, the suffering, for sinners. This all shows us God's wonderful mercy and compassion. It all comes down to God as love, and it is his love alone that can satisfy the hunger of the human heart. One may have all the riches in the world, but if one's heart is not with God, one cannot be truly happy. Eventually every person should come to this understanding. Being made in God's likeness is God's gift. As a result, whether we know it or not, we hunger for the love of God. God is not physical, not of the world of our senses, he is beyond that. Faith gives way to vision; hope gives way to love and possession. Love is what God is. Our love is a participation in the divine. In this life, we can know only through analogy and concept. In the next life, we will know God as he is, seeing him face to face.

Going back more directly to the Rule, there are so many parts with special significance for me. One is the wonderful Prologue and the first word, "Listen." God is a loving Father, and that sets the tone for what follows. St. Benedict begins as a father who says, "Listen!" That listening is the gateway to God's revelation of himself. The listening is not merely listening with the ear but with the heart. It is an awareness with a sensitivity for God and the things of God. The Prologue unfolds the riches of God. Benedict goes on to say, "This is advice from a father who loves you." It's so gentle. The Prologue is a program for one's whole life. To take just those pages alone and live them would be enough.

The chapters on humility are very dear to me. In humility, you know what your condition is, and you also know what your relationship to God is. God calls us to come to the truth, and it is his truth that makes us free, free from bonds of pride. Humility opens us up to God, and we become instruments in his hands. He does the work of sanctification. It's amazing when you think about it. I look back at my own life and I can see here and now the hand of God was at work. The person is left to be free, yet God has his way in spite of one's self.

St. Benedict points out responsibility: "If you see any good in yourself, attribute that to God. What evil you find in yourself, that belongs to you." The world seems not able to see this. The philosophy of the world is self-centeredness; the ego is the center of the universe. The false ego is a lie. The only way to know the truth is to know God.

Chapter 72 is a kind of summing up. It deals with the good zeal of monks. Benedict stresses that each monk should try to be the first to show respect to the other. It reflects our Lord's words, "I came not to be served, but to serve." It is a refrain of love. Benedict goes on to say, "No one is to pursue what he judges better for himself, but instead, what he judges better for someone else." The monk gives to his fellow monks love, to God loving fear, to the abbot unfeigned and humble love. Benedict urges us to prefer nothing whatever to Christ, so that Christ may bring us all to everlasting life. Observance of the commandments may at first be hard and difficult. But as time goes on and the monk advances in virtue and in obedience, he will begin to run on the way of the commandments with an inexpressible delight. I think this is the reason why in regards to the older monks one senses in them a deep peace, a calmness, and an awareness of God's presence. This is the goal to which Benedict points throughout his Rule. In my own life, I experience something of this.

Monasticism was central in forming the civilization of Europe and in preserving knowledge through the ages. It has been a creative force for good down through the centuries. I see and hope for a resurgence in monasticism. And there will be. At the present time, both Catholics and Protestants are taking a special interest in the Rule of St. Benedict and its force for good. When a novice makes the vows, I always see this as a sign of hope. Much like when a baby is born into the world, we say that God still has hope for the world. The newly professed, during the profession ceremony, makes a special prayer of hope, "Accept me, Lord, according to your word and I shall live. Do not disappoint me in my expectation." It is a plea to not get lost along the way. Many people think of monasticism as a high-toned, complex life only for the elite. It isn't. The monastic life is a simple Christian life. The monastics take the gospel as their guide and live it in a committed and serious way.

GLOSSARY

abbey: monastery governed by an abbot or abbess.

abbot/abbess: from the Aramaic "abba," meaning father. The leader of a monastic community of monks. An abbess is a woman leading an abbey of nuns.

adoration: to worship or honor as divine. In the case of the Sisters of Perpetual Adoration, the focus of their adoration is the Blessed Sacrament. An adorer is one who adores.

aspirant: one who is seeking to become a member of a monastic order, before being accepted as a postulant.

diocesan priest: a priest under the authority of a bishop (monastic priests are under the authority of their abbots).

discernment process: the procedure used to determine if one should enter a monastic order. Usually associated with the vocation director.

Divine Office: also called Liturgy of the Hours; the primary focus of a Benedictine community. In the past, monastics gathered seven or eight times a day (the canonical hours) for group prayer; now it is more common to have four meetings: Morning Praise, Noon Prayer, Vespers, and Compline. The prayer's focus is described in the Rule of St. Benedict.

habit: a religious dress worn to symbolize one's monastic status in the church. The habit gives visibility to the monastic values that a person is committed to, and varies for each monastic order.

lay brothers: members of the monastic community who did not take solemn vows. They did not have chapter or voting rights, did not pray the full Divine Office, and performed primarily manual labor. Vatican II abolished this practice.

lectio: also called *lectio divina,* translated as Godly or holy reading. In the teachings of the Rule, each monastic was to spend as much as three hours a day with holy reading; now the time is usually about one hour. While the reading originally focused on Scripture, it can now include related subjects.

motherhouse: a monastery (usually an abbey) from which one or more additional monastic houses have been founded.

mother superior: head of a women's monastic community (term rarely used today).

novice: a person in the formation period of monastic life; in the Benedictine tradition, one year.

novitiate: an institution within the monastery for the development of incoming members, headed by an elder of the community. It is an educational time of learning monastic ideals and spirituality.

oblates: also called associates; individuals who are connected to a monastery but live in the lay world. They attempt to incorporate the teachings of the Rule into their daily lives.

opus Dei: translated as "the work of God" (the Divine Office in the Benedictine tradition).

ora et labora: translated as "prayer and work"—the motto of Benedictine life.

ordination: to be invested (ordained) as a priest.

postulancy: the period that a postulant is required to wait before being admitted to the novitiate.

postulant: a person wishing to join a monastic order.

prior/prioress: a monk/nun appointed by the abbot/abbess to assist in administering the abbey, or heading a dependent house (a priory).

priory: a smaller monastic community, usually dependent on a motherhouse.

profession: to make vows of commitment to God and the monastic order.

Vatican II: initiated by Pope John XXIII, a council of twenty-five hundred Catholic bishops held in Rome from 1962 to 1965 to find ways to renew the church in modern times.

vocation: a divine call to the religious life.

vows: first, or simple, vows are taken after the novice has completed the novitiate. Perpetual, permanent, solemn, or final vows are taken after a second, longer formation period, usually three years after first vows. These vows establish the monastic as a member for life of the community and focus on commitments of poverty, chastity, and obedience.

AMERICAN BENEDICTINE COMMUNITIES

While part of the genius and longevity of the Benedictine tradition lies in the basic independence of each community, monasteries throughout North America have formed federations to support one another. These federations are often based on their European origins and lineage from motherhouses. The following are the primary federations and motherhouses:

Women

The Federation of St. Scholastica [1922]
(St. Joseph's, in St. Marys, Pennsylvania)

The Federation of St. Gertrude [1937]
(Immaculate Conception, in Ferdinand, Indiana)

The Federation of St. Benedict [1947]
(St. Benedict's, in St. Joseph, Minnesota)

Benedictine Sisters of Perpetual Adoration [1874]
(Benedictine Monastery, in Clyde, Missouri)

Men

The American-Cassinese Congregation [1855]
(St. Vincent, in Latrobe, Pennsylvania)

The Swiss-American Federation [1854]
(St. Meinrad, in St. Meinrad, Indiana)

In addition to these federations, there are also some smaller associations as well as nonaligned monasteries.

ACKNOWLEDGMENTS

My foremost thanks to the elders who shared a part of their lives with me, and to all the kind women and men in the thirty Benedictine communities who so warmly welcomed us into their midst. I am deeply indebted to all of them for their generosity and for opening up new paths for me in my life.

My thanks to Sister Kathleen Hickenbotham, Sacred Heart Monastery, Yankton, South Dakota, and Brother Benet Tvedten, Blue Cloud Abbey, Marvin, South Dakota, who both helped to prepare me for my meetings with the elders.

My thanks to Brother Richard Oliver, St. John's Abbey, Collegeville, Minnesota, for kindly providing the Medal of St. Benedict for the book cover.

I would like to thank my friend Legia Spicer who read early drafts of the conversations and made very useful suggestions, and my wife, Sammy, who read many, many drafts of the text and was a great help.

Finally, I would like to express my deep gratitude to my publisher Jan-Erik Guerth, whose guidance has greatly helped shape this book to its final form.

Mark W. McGinnis is an artist, writer, and professor of art at Northern State University, Aberdeen, South Dakota, who has had numerous solo and group art exhibitions across the United States. He is a lay member of the Benedictine community at Blue Cloud Abbey and lives in Hot Springs, South Dakota.